An Internal Family Systems Guide to Recovery from Eating Disorders

Drawing on the evidence-based Internal Family System (IFS) therapy model, *An Internal Family Systems Guide to Recovery from Eating Disorders: Healing Part by Part* addresses the necessity of healing the eating disorder sufferer's three groups of inner "Parts": the Mentors, the Advocates, and the Kids. In order to reconnect to their sense of Self and to achieve an inner balance necessary for recovery, the reader learns to address the unique needs of each of their "Parts." Written in an accessible style, this book combines compassionate examples from the author's client cases and her own recovery with a step-by-step framework for identifying and healing the readers' Parts using the IFS model. Each chapter ends with questions for the reader to answer to further enhance their personal recovery. *An Internal Family Systems Guide to Recovery from Eating Disorders: Healing Part by Part* will be essential to mental health professionals treating clients with eating disorders and to the clients themselves.

Amy Yandel Grabowski, MA, LCPC, ATR, is the founder and director of The Awakening Center, one of the first outpatient eating disorder treatment programs in Chicago, Illinois. She has provided individual psychotherapy and group therapy to women and men with eating disorders for over 30 years and has also led eating disorder support groups for over 20 years. She was trained in the Internal Family Systems therapy model by founder Dr. Richard C. Schwartz and has been a visiting lecturer on eating disorders at Northwestern University, Illinois School of Professional Psychology, National Louis University, and DePaul University. Amy is also a professional member of the National Eating Disorders Association and the International Association of Eating Disorder Professionals and a past member of the Academy of Eating Disorders.

An Internal Family Systems Guide to Recovery from Eating Disorders

Healing Part by Part

Amy Yandel Grabowski

Routledge
Taylor & Francis Group

NEW YORK AND LONDON

First published 2018
by Routledge
711 Third Avenue, New York, NY 10017

and by Routledge
2 Park Square, Milton Park, Abingdon, Oxon, OX14 4RN

Routledge is an imprint of the Taylor & Francis Group, an informa business

© 2018 Amy Yandel Grabowski

The right of Amy Yandel Grabowski to be identified as the author of this work has been asserted by her in accordance with sections 77 and 78 of the Copyright, Designs and Patents Act 1988.

Library of Congress Cataloging in Publication Data
Names: Grabowski, Amy Yandel, author.
Title: An internal family systems guide to recovery from eating disorders : healing part by part / Amy Yandel Grabowski.
Description: First edition. | New York : Routledge, 2017. | Includes bibliographical references.
Identifiers: LCCN 2017006660| ISBN 9781138745209 (hbk : alk. paper) | ISBN 9781138745223 (pbk : alk. paper) | ISBN 9781315180694 (ebk)
Subjects: | MESH: Anorexia Nervosa—therapy | Binge-Eating Disorder—therapy | Bulimia—therapy | Family Therapy | Self Concept | Personal Narratives | Case Reports
Classification: LCC RC552.A5 | NLM WM 175 | DDC 616.85/262—dc23
LC record available at https://lccn.loc.gov/2017006660

ISBN: 978-1-138-74520-9 (hbk)
ISBN: 978-1-138-74522-3 (pbk)
ISBN: 978-1-315-18069-4 (ebk)

Typeset in Sabon
by Swales & Willis Ltd, Exeter, Devon, UK

To my sister Terri. You showed me what true courage is. I miss you every day!

And to my daughter, Alison. You give me hope for future generations by living each day as a strong and independent young woman with body love and acceptance!

"What is Real?" asked the Rabbit one day, when they were lying side by side near the nursery fender, before Nana came to tidy the room. "Does it mean having things that buzz inside you and a stick-out handle?"

"Real isn't how you are made," said the Skin Horse. "It's a thing that happens to you. When a child loves you for a long, long time, not just to play with, but really loves you, then you become Real."

"Does it hurt?" asked the Rabbit.

"Sometimes," said the Skin Horse, for he was always truthful. "When you are Real you don't mind being hurt."

"Does it happen all at once, like being wound up," he asked, "or bit by bit?"

"It doesn't happen all at once," said the Skin Horse. "You become. It takes a long time. That's why it doesn't often happen to people who break easily, or have sharp edges, or who have to be carefully kept. Generally, by the time you are Real, most of your hair has been loved off, and your eyes drop out and you get loose in the joints and very shabby. *But these things don't matter at all, because once you are Real you can't be ugly, except to people who don't understand.*"

The Velveteen Rabbit
Margery Williams
© 1922 Heinemann, London

"A journey of a thousand miles begins with a single step."

Lao-Tzu, *Tao Te Ching*, trans. by J. Legge (1891)

Contents

Illustrations

Figures

Table

Foreword

Reading Amy Yandel Grabowski's book *An Internal Family Systems Guide to Recovery from Eating Disorders: Healing Part by Part* gave me great joy because she uses a wonderful treatment method which has allowed many to recover completely from eating disorders.

Amy describes Subconscious Parts which, to be effective, need to work as a team directed by a stronger "Self." Amy categorizes these Parts according to their function as Mentor, Advocate, and Kid. You don't have them? Think again!

Here is a simple explanation that might convince you. Think back to when you were a child alone in the kitchen with the cookie jar in plain sight and reach. Did you hear your mother's voice loud and clear, "No cookies before dinner!"? Did another voice say, "She'll never know!"? Was there a scuffle between the two voices? Was the battle long or short? Who won?

Amy says Wise decisions are made only when our Self is in charge. As we develop and grow the conflicts among our Parts become more complicated and harder to resolve. A Wise decision maker is needed therefore, a strongly developed Self. When the Self is sacrificed, unhealthy behaviors come into place: starving, bingeing, alcohol, drugs, self-effacement, and self-hate. This usurps one's ability to develop into an assured, confident individual who can take actions and make decisions necessary for a satisfying life.

Why do I believe that establishing Self and working with our Parts is such a good idea? The first reason is Amy's experience of complete recovery by this therapeutic mode. The second originates from my own exploration of and belief in various treatments for eating disorders. At a professional conference, Dr Richard Schwartz presented on Internal Family Systems Therapy. "Ho hum, another family therapy variant" was my view, which changed to complete astonishment as the patient being presented on video showed total focused attention to the problem under consideration.

A large number of patients report complete recovery from eating disorders with Internal Family Systems Therapy. Amy uses the same approach and most convincing is Amy's conviction that her own therapist's use of these methods enabled her to achieve complete recovery.

Many patients and therapists will now be able to utilize the concepts expressed so clearly by Amy Yandel Grabowski in her fascinating book.

Vivian Hansen Meehan, RN, DSc
Founder and former President of ANAD

Preface

There is an abundance of books and theories about eating disorders and recovery. In fact, I borrow bits and pieces from many of them. This book is based on my own recovery, personal research, readings, professional trainings, and observations from 30 years of working with men and women with eating disorders. To paraphrase holistic author Dr Deepak Chopra, "I'm just singing in the shower. If anyone wants to listen, that's fine with me."

In the 30 years that I have been helping clients recover from eating disorders, I have seen many changes. In 1986, my clients were typically young, white, straight, cis-females from middle- or upper-class Christian or Jewish families. Now, at The Awakening Center, we see clients of all ages, ethnicities, races, socio-economic levels, religions, sexual orientations, and gender identities. Not only are more diverse clients coming forward to get help but, unfortunately, eating disorders are spreading into all corners of society.

In this book you will read about aspects of my story along with the experiences of many of my clients. Some examples, such as Bethany, are composites of many clients, while others are direct quotes from my case notes. To protect the privacy of those who told their stories, all names have been changed. For simplicity's sake, I use the female pronoun rather than the cumbersome her/his or she/he, except in examples that are about male clients. I only include personal information about a client if it is pertinent to the eating disorder or recovery process.

The vast majority of my clients have been trauma survivors, especially sexual abuse trauma. I do not want to belittle the enormity of healing the wounds of sexual abuse in the small amount that is devoted to it in this book. For those of you who are sexual abuse survivors, your journey will be painful and may take longer. But I want to reassure you that it is completely possible for you to recover fully as well. I recommend that you work with a caring therapist who has special training and experience working with sexual abuse survivors.

This book is intended for those who know they have an eating disorder or who struggle with disordered eating. Many physical and mental illnesses have symptoms that can mimic an eating disorder. I urge you to see a medical doctor to rule out these illnesses before embarking upon a recovery program.

If you have any questions, comments, suggestions or feedback, I would love to hear from you.

Namastè,

Amy Yandel Grabowski, MA, LCPC, ATR
The Awakening Center
3523 N Lincoln Ave
Chicago, IL 60657
(773) 929-6262
www.awakeningcenter.net

Acknowledgments

If you are or were one of my clients, and an example in this book sounds familiar to you then, yes, it's probably you. Because I can't thank you by name, my inclusion of examples from your journey is offered with deep gratitude. I consider it an honor to have been invited to guide you during your recovery journey. This book could not have been written without each and every one of you.

My special thanks go to three incredible women who lent me their Self-energy when my Exiles were mired in self-doubt and the procrastinating Troublemakers took over:

- Erin Stitzel, MA, LPC, from The Awakening Center, who wrote the questions for the ends of each chapter and who worked with me, sometimes daily, when I was stuck;
- Arlene Brennan who supported and encouraged me chapter by chapter;
- Nancy Hall, MA, LPC, from The Awakening Center, who patiently edited this book over and over and took it from a rough stone and turned it into a polished gem.

Thanks also to:

- Eric Zorn and the Someday Is Now Society who in 2001 got me started writing this book one half an hour a day.
- The members of the North Suburban Writers Group: Diane, Judy, Steve, and especially Paul, who read so many versions of this book they probably know it by heart.
- Rachel Baker, MA, LPC, who posed for the pictures in Chapter 1.
- And any friends and family members who ever inquired about me, encouraged me, supported me, and cajoled me into finishing this book.
- And to my husband Greg who never doubted that this book would be written!

1 Two Halves of Recovery

I know you. However, chances are great that I have never met you. I know you because I've walked in your shoes. I've been where you are now. I did what you do. I thought your thoughts, and I suffered your pain. I struggled with your confusion. I experienced that hollow emptiness inside. I experienced that life-is-spinning-out-of-control feeling you often do now. I tried to find the answers too. And I relapsed many times until I found both halves of recovery.

My Story

My descent into the dark abyss of eating disorders began in my early 20s, although I don't think I ever had a "normal" relationship with food or my body. As far back as I could remember – even as a child – I was uncomfortable in my own skin. I found it painful to be me; I often felt completely out of control and miserable in every aspect of my very existence. Growing up, I was sure I lacked some fundamentally important quality that others seemed to naturally have. I became good at acting "as if." But I was afraid others would find out that I didn't have whatever it was that I lacked, even though I didn't know what it was.

After college, on the outside I looked like I had everything – a good job, a stable marriage; but on the inside I felt completely hollow, empty, defective, and full of self-loathing. I couldn't stand myself, and I was sure that no one else could stand me either. Then, one unremarkable day, I stumbled upon what felt like an answer: a diet! Focusing all my attention on losing weight, in any way possible, distracted me from my problems and made life seem bearable for a while.

But, after a while, the eating disorder took over my world. My life revolved around thinking about what I was going to eat, when I would eat it, what I weighed, and worrying that I would lose control. The stress of trying not to fall back on my symptoms and behaviors made it worse; the only way I could cope was by falling back on my symptoms and behaviors. Life was terrifying, like walking a tightrope over a deep chasm. I felt trapped, and I had no idea how to get out.

After battling my eating disorder for what seemed an eternity, I gave up. Feeling completely hopeless, despondent, and beaten, I checked into a hospital where, I was disappointed to learn, I was the only patient with an eating disorder on the unit. Dr O., the therapist assigned to me, was kind and caring, and we got along fine. But from the start it was apparent she didn't know much about treating eating disorders.

Meeting My Parts

I was the ideal patient; I cheerfully went to all the therapy groups and said what I thought the therapists wanted to hear. After two weeks, feeling no better than when I checked in, I still struggled with feelings of hopelessness and despair. In a session with Dr O., I finally allowed a crack in my cheerful façade and tearfully told her how I was really feeling. "I'm really scared. A part of me feels really hopeless, like I'll never be able to recover. What if I just can't do it? What if I can't beat this?"

"The Part of you who feels hopeless, what is that Part like?" Dr O. gently asked.

Closing my eyes, I described a Little Girl with a long brown ponytail wearing blue pajamas. She was really young, sitting on the floor in the kitchen of my childhood home, clinging to her dog. She was scared and crying.

"Is there another Part who wants to get better?" Dr O. asked.

Skeptically, I concentrated for a while. Surprisingly, a Woman appeared to me, standing confidently, wearing a flowing, angelic, aqua-colored gown. With Dr O.'s prompting, I asked the Woman if she would help me take care of the Little Girl. The Woman nodded and smiled.

For the rest of the hour, Dr O. and I conversed with the Woman. She promised to use her inner resources to help me recover. By the end of the session, the Little Girl was calm; she was no longer scared. For the first time in a long, long time, I felt taken care of. I didn't feel alone.

Thus began my journey of working with my inner Parts. Dr O. and I discovered many Parts. Together, we had countless dialogues with, and among, all the Parts and, slowly, learned all their stories. Over time, the Parts revealed what they were trying to do for me and what they needed from the Woman. As they felt heard, they stopped fighting with one another. The Woman, the Parts, and I became a team.

Most importantly, I found the Woman – she was my "Self," a deep inner feeling of strength, peace, and wisdom. For the first time in my life, I felt at peace. I was the person I was meant to be. I felt real!

Both Halves of Recovery

At this point you may be wondering, "What is this magical thing that gave you peace, because I want it!" Or you might be skeptical: "How is your approach any different from all the other books already written about recovery?"

To put it briefly, I couldn't recover until I had both halves of recovery in place. As long as I concentrated on only the food, eating, and weight, my attempts at recovery crumbled under my feet. Fixing the food, eating, and weight and not finding your Self is like taking aspirin for a headache that is caused by a brain tumor. The symptoms and behaviors will keep coming back until the fundamental causes are resolved.

What are the two halves of recovery? Simply put, one half represents making peace with food, eating, weight, and the body. But the other half represents finding your Self and making peace with your Parts. You'll learn more about the Self and Parts in Chapter 2.

If you address one half of your recovery – only the eating, food, and weight – you will always be tense, on edge, rigid, strained, and uncomfortable. Eating will always be a struggle. To feel what I mean, put your hands together so that your fingertips are touching and your fingers are curved, like you are holding a large softball (see Figure 1.1). Pay attention to how this feels. How long could you hold your hands like this? Most people find it comfortable, fairly easy to do. Both hands can relax because they support each other.

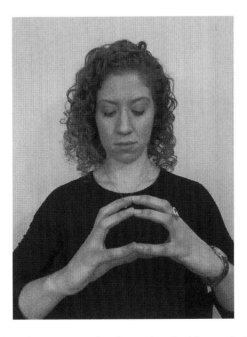

Figure 1.1 Two hands support each other (printed with permission of Rachel Baker).

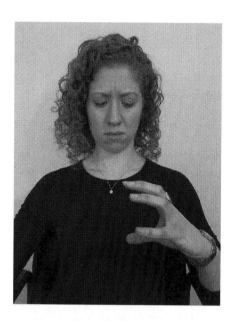

Figure 1.2 One hand tense without support (printed with permission of Rachel Baker).

Figure 1.3 Two hands can relax with support (printed with permission of Rachel Baker).

Now, keeping your left hand in the same curved position, take the right hand away (see Figure 1.2). Now what do you notice? Without the support of the right hand, your left hand must tense to keep its position. The fingers may start to shake. Are you feeling pressure in your hand or wrist? Tingling? It would be uncomfortable to hold your hand like this for too long.

Bring your hands back together again as in Figure 1.3. Notice what happens. The left hand instantly relaxes. It becomes easy again because the two hands balance and support each other.

The same is true with the two halves of recovery. If you fix only the eating, food, and weight half, tension and discomfort remain. But when your Self and your Parts are at peace, then eating, food, and weight can be easy and in balance as well. You need both halves of recovery to relax and feel complete.

Food, Eating, and Weight

Concerns about food, eating, and weight can cause so much anguish and are often what prompt clients to seek therapy. When I ask a new client for her therapy goals, she says, "I want to stop bingeing and purging," "I don't want to eat this way," or "I want to be normal around food." She will go on to tell me all the ways in which she has tried to control her food, eating, and weight.

Thinking Weight Loss Is the Answer

The first thing my client Bethany did to control her food, eating, and weight was try to lose weight. You know what I'm talking about, don't you? You may look at weight loss as the answer to your problems. You may think that if you could only reach a certain number on the scale, then all would be well in your life. As you know, that number never appears. No matter what the scale reads, even with drastic measures such as cosmetic surgery or liposuction, you never feel OK inside. That little voice inside your head continues to say, "Maybe if you lose five more pounds." Even when you appear emaciated to others, you still feel fat, not good enough, empty, and defective, and full of shame inside and out.

You may feel the conflict just like my client Michelle described:

> When I try to stop purging, I know it's healthier for me. But the voice in my head starts telling me that if I were thinner I'd be happy. I know it's not the answer, because I remember when I was thinner I wasn't happy. I was miserable. But the voice insists in order to be happy I have to lose weight. I can't win for trying!

Trying Food Combinations as the Answer

Or maybe you've been drawn to certain food combinations looking for the answer to fix your eating disorder or to "control" your weight.

- "They say less carbs and more protein is the way to go."
- "If I eliminate all fats, then I'll be able to eat normally."
- "I must be addicted to sugar. I should avoid all sweets to be OK."
- "Maybe I need to avoid gluten."

But, even as you search for the answer among the many different foods out there, deep inside you know that food is not the real issue.

Trying Exercise as an Answer

So, if food is not the answer, then perhaps the answer is . . . exercise. Maybe, like my client Tanya, you need to run or work out every day, no matter what. During one of our sessions together, Tanya admitted to running along Chicago's lakefront path when the wind-chill was 60 degrees below zero. What? Is she crazy? Why would she put herself in a physically dangerous situation like that? Her answer was, "I *had* to! If I don't run, I feel fat." Ironically, Tanya felt fat anyway.

Recovery Language Focuses on Food, Eating, and Weight

Even the labels "anorexia nervosa" (which means "nervous loss of appetite"), "bulimia" ("ox-hunger"), "compulsive overeating", and "binge eating disorder" emphasize the food, eating, and weight half of the eating disorder. The language from some organizations reinforces this notion as well: "You're always one bite away from your next binge." "You can never recover, you can only be abstinent." I remember feeling very hopeless hearing this, "If I have to fight with myself every day for the rest of my life, then why bother? It's easier to just stay sick."

Very well-meaning friends and family members also don't get it. They think, "You have an *eating* disorder. So fix the *eating* and you'll be OK." Trying to be helpful, they say, "All you have to do is eat three meals a day." "Just eat when you're hungry and stop when you're full." "Don't be so selfish, there are much more important things in life to think about." Personally, my least favorite is, "Just stop. Don't do it anymore!" As if the recipient of this advice is supposed to hit her forehead with insight and gratefully exclaim, "Wow! I never thought of that before! Thanks so much for your advice. I'm all better now! Let's go have lunch!"

If only it were that simple.

My Early Attempts at Recovery

I also fell for these common misconceptions. During my first attempt at recovery, all of my time and energy was spent controlling my food and stopping any food-related symptom: I ate well-balanced, pre-planned, normal meals and I weighed a pre-determined "normal" weight. Even though I received some praise from others "You are recovered!" inside I still felt chaotic, hollow, empty, defective, ashamed, and just not good enough. Each day was a struggle, but I assumed that's how all "normal" people felt. Now that I had recovered, I thought everything was going to be perfect. The first time life threw a zinger my way, I freaked out.

"Why was this happening to me?" I wondered. "Why were the people in my life acting this way?" This made no sense to me. I had stopped my eating disorder, right? I ate normally, right? I looked normal, right? So why was life throwing curveballs at me? What was wrong with me? I didn't know what to do and not knowing how to handle this stress made me feel more out of control. After a few more weeks of struggling to be normal, of trying to manage my life by controlling my eating and by looking normal, the eating disorder symptoms returned. And I must admit I welcomed them back like old friends.

If you fix only the food, eating, and weight without finding your Self and making peace with your Parts, each day will be a constant struggle – like the one tensed hand. In order to achieve total recovery, you need to establish a firm sense of Self, know who you really are inside, and be in harmony with all your Parts, while at the same time making peace with your food and your body.

Inner Emptiness

The majority of people who have an eating disorder feel out of control and chaotic, hollow and empty, and full of shame. They do not know who they really are. Having an eating disorder gives them something to base their identity on: "I am a bulimic." (Or "an anorexic" or "a compulsive eater.") Many of my clients have expressed the following worries:

- "If I give up my eating disorder, who will I be?"
- "If I'm not the skinniest person in the room, I won't be special."
- "I won't know who I am."
- "It feels like I have to give up the script of my life if I recover."

If your eating disorder is who you are, then giving it up means uprooting your very identity. This may feel dangerous.

When I was a child, as far back as I can remember, I felt like something vital was missing; inside I felt scooped out and hollow like a plastic doll. If you cut me in half, I felt like I'd be full of foul-smelling, black, tarry gunk. I feared if others really knew me deep down, they'd discover my secret shame, though even I didn't know what it was. I just always felt "not good enough." So I had to spend all my time pretending. I was good at acting normal, but I was always anxious and on guard, terrified that someone would discover the real me, and sure that I'd be rejected and abandoned.

Many of my clients have described the inner emptiness and shame as well:

- "I have no idea who I am. I know who others tell me to be, but without them I would be nothing."
- "I feel disconnected, alone, hopeless, scared, lost in a meaningless void. This void sparks an inner panic, a monstrous sense of impending doom."
- "It feels like a profound core wound, as if I knew I was not wanted and not loved even before I was born."

Since it feels as if there is nothing on the inside of you, the outside of you – your size, shape, and appearance – becomes crucially important.

The Sacrifice of the Self

Where did the inner emptiness and shame come from? The inner emptiness is the hole where your Self should be. So, what happened to it? In a nutshell, a long time ago – consciously or unconsciously – your Self was sacrificed. It may have been chipped away bit by bit over time, cracked apart like freezing and thawing a rock, blown apart all at once like a stick of dynamite, or a combination of all three. We will explore these in detail in Chapter 3.

Your Self is who you are, the one who is in charge of your Parts, and who leads you through your life. Without a Self in charge, the Parts chaotically take over and fight with each other for control. Without a sense of Self, you feel powerless. You lack a sense of control over what happens to you or how you respond to life's challenges. In many situations, your first reaction is to grab onto something that seems to give you a feeling of control (Food! Eating! Weight!), but that control is just an illusion and its effect is temporary.

Cognitive Behavioral Therapy (CBT) and the Self

You may be confused by now. "I was told CBT was the treatment model of choice for eating disorders." Yes, CBT is quick and easy to learn; many have made significant strides in a short amount of time. Because of insurance limits on hospital stays, many treatment centers rely heavily on it.

But, if a Young Part of you truly believes deep inside "I am just not lovable," then saying, "That is all-or-nothing thinking. There are some people who love me, therefore I am lovable" will just feel like empty words. Young Parts, who hold your negative core beliefs, have to be healed emotionally – in the amygdala, a part of the limbic system of your brain – not just cognitively in the prefrontal cortex. To paraphrase internationally recognized trauma expert Bessel van der Kolk MD, your prefrontal cortex does not communicate with the amygdala. You cannot think your way out of your emotions.

Unless you find your sense of Self, emotionally heal your Young Parts, and get all your Parts in harmony you will eventually relapse and slide right back into your negative thinking and eating disordered ways. After you have established a firm sense of Self and your Young Parts have experienced emotional healing, CBT can be a very useful addition to your recovery toolbox.

Finding the Self and Healing the Parts

The answer is not so clear-cut anymore. If you don't count calories, continually exercise, or focus on your appearance and weight, what do you do to recover? How does one actually recover?

You will learn how to reclaim your Self – to fill the emptiness inside; this will be covered in Chapter 4. Your Self is the person you were meant to be. Your Self is a deep-seated, compassionate, and calm feeling of personal strength and wisdom you can tap into at any time. Your Self fills you inside; you feel solid. Like the foundation of a pyramid, the stability and strength of your Self is always with you, no matter what.

In Chapters 5 through 7 you will learn to establish peace with your various Parts so you can live each day in harmony and cooperation with your Self. A large portion of recovery will be to emotionally heal shame from your negative core beliefs, what you hold deep inside about who you think you are, and resolving all beliefs that are inaccurate, outdated or just plain wrong.

In Chapter 8 you will find a personal meaning to your life; finding where you fit in the bigger picture. Being able to put experiences into perspective and knowing what is important and what is trivial. Learning to live life fully with your values and ethics in a fulfilling manner.

Then, in Chapter 9, you'll put it all together – how can you apply this to your everyday life, especially in relation to food, eating, and weight, and how to maintain your recovery.

I picture the two halves of recovery as a three dimensional yin-yang. When we put the two halves together, we can live our lives in peace. The answer lies in finding your Self, the person you were meant to be.

Questions to Enhance Your Personal Recovery

Find a quiet time and some privacy to ponder the following questions. You may want to journal what you learn about yourself. I encourage you to share your answers with your therapist.

1   When reading this chapter, did you notice different Parts that popped up for you? Young, old, ageless? Male, female, both, neither? Loud, quiet? Submissive, aggressive?
2   Is there a Part of you that feels like you'll never be able to recover? What is this Part like?
3   Are there one or more other Parts of you who want to get better? Describe these Parts.
4   Do you sometimes feel empty inside? What are your reactions and thoughts about this emptiness?
5   Thinking about your own recovery, which half have you been more focused on? Eating, food, and weight or finding peace with your Self and Parts? How has your recovery felt so far?
6   Once you have recovered, what do you envision for your life? What in your life would look or feel different so you know you have achieved Self-acceptance and peace?

Note

To find an Internal Family Systems therapist in your area or for more information about Internal Family Systems Therapy contact: The Center for Self Leadership, PO Box 3969, Oak Park, IL 60303. (708) 383-2659, www.selfleadership.org

Reference

Schwartz, Richard C. (1995) *Internal Family Systems Therapy*. New York, NY: Guilford Press

2 The Conductor and the Orchestra

Before I introduce you to your Self and your Parts, I want to tell you another piece of my story.

Because of my recovery, I decided to change careers to become a therapist. I wanted to help others find inner strength, peace, and happiness too. All through graduate school I tried to fit the way I had recovered in my own therapy to the various therapeutic models I was taught. While each of them had valuable aspects, none of them fit quite right. They all lacked the magical quality I felt during that therapy session when I met the Woman.

Nevertheless, I began my career as a therapist, finding I had an intuitive way of knowing what my clients' needs were. I was often frustrated, though, when I tried to explain to other professionals about working with clients' different Parts. I knew what I was doing was helping them, but I felt discouraged that others could not see the validity of this approach.

Two years later, I attended a professional conference for the treatment of eating disorders. As I look back on that pivotal day, I now believe fate was actively steering me in the direction I needed to take. The workshop I wanted to attend was cancelled, so I went to hear Dr Richard C. Schwartz speak about Internal Family Systems (IFS) Therapy.

Dr Schwartz spoke about his work with clients struggling with bulimia. He explained how they discovered distinct inner personalities, which they often referred to as "Parts". My jaw dropped. As he described the different groups of Parts, I knew I finally found what I was looking for.

After the workshop, I approached Dr Schwartz. "How do you know this? Where did you find this way of working?"

"My clients taught it to me," he answered.

"This is how I recovered. I didn't know others were doing this too," I explained excitedly.

"It's amazing, isn't it?" he replied with a knowing smile.

My subsequent work with clients with eating disorders has been greatly influenced by my training in the IFS Therapy model. I love how IFS is flexible and adaptive; it is not pathologizing, instead it is strengths-based. The model itself has evolved greatly since I was trained by Dr Schwartz in the late 1980s and has been recognized by the US government's Substance Abuse and Mental Health Services Administration

Table 2.1 Official IFS terms compared with my terms for Self and Parts.

IFS terms:	My terms for Part when stuck in extreme or negative role:	My terms for Part when in positive role or when in balance:
Self	–	Self Wise One Within The Wise One
Manager	Bully	Mentor
Firefighter	Troublemaker	Advocate
Exile	Exile	Kid

(SAMHSA) as an evidence-based practice. Over the years, I have taken the official IFS terms and put my own spin on them, making them more user-friendly for my clients (see Table 2.1).

In IFS therapy we explore the various inner personalities that we refer to as Parts: "A Part of me wants to go out with my friends, but another Part knows I need to stay home to finish my report." It is normal to have Parts. Everyone you know has them – even "normal" eaters have Parts. (I jokingly wonder if there are any "normal" eaters in the United States; maybe a few are hiding in the mountains of Idaho.)

Just like your family, your Parts interact and react to one another. You may be aware of them through your thoughts, feelings, beliefs, and inner dialog. When your Parts are out of balance, it may feel noisy and chaotic, like your Parts cannot get along.

So how do we quiet all this noise and chaos? In addition to our Parts we have a Self, which I often refer to as the Wise One Within. The Self is the one in charge of all the Parts, helping them to work together in harmony and balance.

When I try to describe the Self, words seem inadequate, like trying to describe an exact shade of a color to someone who hasn't seen it. The Self is a feeling, deep inside, of being OK, no matter what. The Self is a quiet peaceful place of wisdom that holds all the answers. When you are in your Self, Self-energy, or Self-leadership, you know who you are and what is right for you. It's not a thinking kind of knowing but a gut intuition.

To me, my Self is like the base of a pyramid: solid, secure, and constant. It's a core feeling that is always there. It endures. It's a belief deep in my body that I truly can handle whatever comes along; that I really am good enough deep inside.

My clients have described the Self in similar ways:

- "My Self is like a column of strength inside my body I can tap into at any time."
- "It's a spiritual channel that allows Wisdom to speak to me."
- "I feel quiet, calm, wise and peaceful inside."

The Orchestra

In his book *Internal Family Systems Therapy*, Dr Schwartz compares the relationship between the Self and the Parts with an orchestra. Picture for a moment a professional orchestra and listen to the beautiful harmony of a symphony. The Self is the conductor and all the Parts are the many instruments. Just as an orchestra needs all the different instruments to achieve the richness and depth of the music, we need all our different Parts to fully experience life.

If you think about what an orchestra does, it's incredible. Numerous musicians playing different instruments, all performing different lines of music, at the same time, in rhythm, and in tune, together. How do they perform so beautifully? They follow the lead of the conductor – just as how the Parts can work together when they are guided by the Self.

The conductor has a deep love, understanding, and appreciation for each of the musicians. The musicians respect and trust the leadership of the conductor. If a musician has a problem, the conductor stops the orchestra to give them needed attention. When the problem is resolved, the orchestra resumes playing.

Similarly, the Self appreciates and trusts the Parts, and they, in turn, listen to and respect the judgment of the Self. When one of the Parts needs help, the Self gives it guidance until the Parts can find harmony again.

The 11 Cs of Self

The Self has many qualities that begin with the letter C (see Figure 2.1). The Self is Centered and grounded, Calm and peaceful. The Self holds our Compassion, a loving, empathic nurturance towards ourselves, our Parts, and other people. The Self also feels Courage and Confidence, and possesses the Clarity needed to handle situations. Using its qualities of Curiosity and Creativity, the Self helps the Parts resolve problems that may arise. We are able to be Current – in the present moment – when we are in our Self. The Self has the Capacity for objectivity – the ability to step back and observe our Parts, other people, or ourselves, without criticism or judgment. And through the Self we Connect to who we are, to our Parts, to other people, and to a Higher Power or to our place in the bigger picture of life.

The Self is connected to the wisdom of our bodies and sends us signals – hunger, fullness, thirst, and our body's need for rest and movement. Our body also tells us its nutritional needs for protein, carbohydrates, fruits and vegetables, and, yes, even fats. When we respond to these signals with Compassion and Curiosity, then we can be healthy.

The Three Groups of Parts

In the language of the IFS Therapy, the Parts are divided into three categories: the Manager, the Exile, and the Firefighter. Over the years,

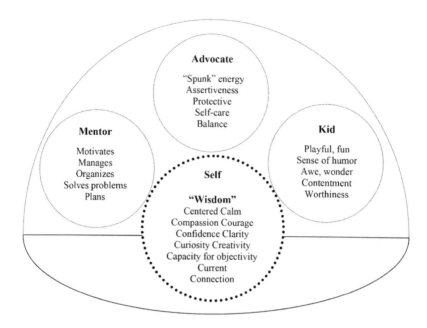

Figure 2.1 Self and Parts in balance.

I have adapted the names, using ones that I have found to be more descriptive of how the Parts are experienced by my clients: the Mentors, Kids, and Advocates. You may have several Parts with slightly different roles in each group. The descriptions that follow are guidelines, not rigid rules. As you read about the different Parts, please trust your own inner experience. If I say Mentors often feel adult in age, but one of your Mentors feels young to you, so be it. Please don't try to force your Parts to fit.

In Figure 2.1 you'll notice the Parts are drawn in circles to symbolize that, when in balance, they are centered and grounded, like the Self. The dotted lines suggest that communication between the Parts is open.

The Mentors

Mentors often feel adult in age and are usually experienced in the head as thoughts. Mentors want you to find fulfillment and meaning in life. They motivate you to move forward and learn, grow, and be the best you can be. Mentors organize, plan, problem-solve, and manage your day-to-day life. They are very productive and promote action. When you eat, the Mentors are concerned with good nutrition and well-being. They encourage you to exercise to be fit and healthy.

The Kids

While the Mentors keep you focused on tasks and achievement, the Kids make life enjoyable along the way. Kid Parts usually feel young and, more often than not, are experienced as emotions and sensations in the body. Kids are fun and playful; your sense of humor comes from the Kids. They possess awe and the wonder of life. Self-worth, contentment, and a love of life can come from the Kids. They eat for fun and enjoyment and love to move for fun.

The Advocates

The Advocates can be any age, but often remind me of the spunk and energy of adolescence. They speak to you through your thoughts as well as through your body. The Advocates push you to take care of yourself, stand up for yourself, and protect yourself. They help you to find balance in your life. When you eat, the Advocates listen to the signals of your body and help balance the need for nutrition and health with the need for fun and enjoyment. The Advocates also balance exercise and movement for fitness and fun with rest and relaxation.

What Parts Want from the Self

The Parts want three things from the Self. They want the Self to:

1   Listen to them; it's important that all Parts feel heard.
2   Appreciate what they are trying to do for you.
3   Take care of them when they need it and in the way they need it.

When the Parts feel heard, appreciated, and taken care of by the Self you feel a feeling of peace, inner harmony and cooperation within.

There are four important points you must know about the Parts. First, you may be disappointed to learn, we can't get rid of any of our Parts. You may have already tried to disown some of your Parts and so you know it doesn't work. If they sense you are trying to eliminate them, they will fight harder to get their way. If you ignore them or try to shut them up, instead of making them quieter, they get louder and even nastier in order to be heard. (Remember, the first thing the Parts want is to be heard.)

Second, each of the Parts exists on a continuum. On one end of the continuum, the Parts are healthy and in balance. When healthy and in balance, the Parts cooperate with one another. As the Parts move toward the other end of the continuum, they get more and more extreme in their thoughts, feelings, attitudes, and behaviors. They get stuck, out of balance, not harmonious, and uncooperative with each other.

Third, all of the Parts have a positive intention at the root of all their actions, feelings, and thoughts. When the Parts cooperate and work together, their positive intentions are easy to figure out. But when a Part's behavior is extreme and is stuck in negative ways of expressing its needs, the positive intention is hard to find. When a Part gets nasty, often there will be a negative outcome, no matter how positive the intention may be.

Fourth, your Parts think, feel, behave, and react just like their real-life counterparts. That means that if a Part is 6 years old it will think, feel, and act just a like a real child of that age, even though you may be decades older.

Parts without Self Leadership

If the Self is in charge and the Parts feel heard, appreciated and taken care of, you'll experience them as calm, balanced, and in harmony. However, if the Self has been sacrificed, leadership is lost, and the Parts fight with each other for control. Instead of a professional orchestra, picture a junior high school band when the teacher doesn't show up.

What did you imagine when you read that? Did you hear beautiful harmony? No – just a lot of noise. Without anyone in charge, chaos and anarchy rule. A bully grabs the piccolo and throws it in the tuba. An anxious kid worries, "Oh, we're all going to get in trouble! We should keep practicing anyway." A rebel shouts, "Who cares! I never liked you anyway, get out of here!" Then the drummer plays as loud as he can to drown out everyone else. What happened to the beautiful harmonious cooperative symphony? It's lost. It's just noise and chaos.

The fighting among your own Parts may feel just as noisy and chaotic as that junior high school band. When your Self was sacrificed, a Part took over as leader – the Pseudo-Self. But this Part is not the Self and doesn't have its calming ability; and the other Parts don't respect its judgment. Some Parts become very anxious. Others rebel: "Why are you in charge? You can't tell me what to do! I want to be in charge!" Inside you feel chaos, anxiety, noise, and anarchy.

The cooperation is gone; each of the Parts has their own agenda, which they feel is more important than any other Part's agenda.

The Parts need a capable leader to keep them working together. They need the Self.

"Ed"

Many of my clients have named their Eating Disorder "Ed." It is very important to know that your eating disorder is not just one Part but rather the thoughts, feelings, beliefs, and behaviors of all the Parts. Deep inside you know this to be true. If you ask yourself, "Why do I binge [or starve or purge]?" you will come up with lots of different answers. "Because I'm angry – or lonely – or hurt."

As you read further, we will look at the Parts when they are extreme, and I will explain the differences and roles that add up to the complete picture of your eating disorder.

Finding the Self

So where is your Self? Some worry that it's nonexistent; but the Self is just hidden away under layers of Parts, so many layers that it may seem like it's not there at all. But it is there. In another of Dr Schwartz's analogies, the Self is like the President of the United States. If the United States were under attack, the President is whisked away to a safe place for his or her own protection. After the crisis, he or she returns to the leadership role and everyone gets back to normal. When your Self was sacrificed it was hidden away for its own protection. Our job is to find it and return it to a leadership role.

When Parts Have No Leader

Let's look at what happens to the Parts without the Self (see Figure 2.2). Without a sense of Self, you feel hollow, empty, directionless, lost, full of

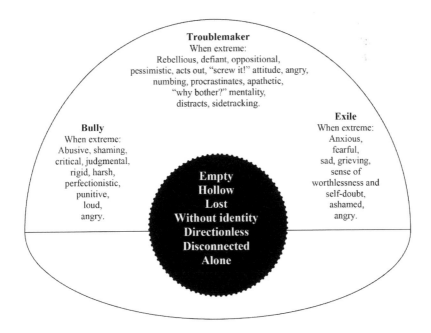

Figure 2.2 Lack of Self and Parts out of balance.

shame, and totally alone. You don't know who you are, what you enjoy, what you believe in, or where you are going in your life. You lose any meaningful connection with others or with a higher power or your place in the bigger picture of life.

The Exiles

When the Kids become extreme, I call them the Exiles. Without the Self's soothing, reassuring presence, the Exiles feel frightened. Realizing they are alone, that there is no one to take care of them, they become anxious. Because they are young and inexperienced they don't know how to handle situations; they may freeze or try to hide or escape.

The Exiles are full of shame and self-doubt, and they feel worthless. When angry, they lash out at others, or, more often, they turn that anger back on themselves, "I should have known better. What's wrong with me? I'm not good enough."

The Exiles collect traumatic memories and negative messages from people in the past and turn them into the core belief system, the definition of who you think you are deep inside. The other Parts rally around to lock the Exiles away to keep you from feeling uncomfortable intense emotions and painful memories. The more traumatic the memories, the more extreme the other Parts work to keep you from getting near the closet where the Exiles' memories and feelings are banished. Locked away, the Exiles feel alone, despondent, hopeless, worthless, ashamed, and angry.

The Exiles turn to food, seeking comfort and companionship and to pacify their needs. They prefer the soothing foods of childhood. If they are not running away to avoid their feelings, they often don't want to move at all.

The Bullies

When the Mentors become extreme I call them the Bullies. They are often the Pseudo-Self I mentioned in a previous section. Bullies are critical, judgmental, perfectionistic, punitive, loud, and angry. They rush in to take care of any situation but, because the Bullies do not possess the soothing, reassuring wisdom of the Self, their care-taking is not what the Exiles need or want: "Buck up! Stop being such a crybaby! No one else is acting like this. Why don't you just get over it?" The Exiles, looking for soothing and reassurance, become more agitated and fearful when the Bullies yell. The Bullies react to the anxiety with more criticism, which elicits more anxiety, which elicits more perfectionism . . . . Round and round they go.

Extreme Bullies set up very rigid rules about exercise and eating, "You must exercise three hours every day – no matter how tired or in pain you are.

You can only have xxx calories today, no more! And you must only eat wholegrain, organic, fat-free, gluten-free foods. And nothing after 7 p.m." The Bullies also use eating or starving to express anger or to punish either you or someone in your life, "You want cookies! You're going to get cookies! You're going to regret you ever wanted cookies!" Or, "I'll show them. You won't eat until they're sorry they did this to you."

The Troublemakers

In the extreme, Advocates become Troublemakers who may take on several roles.

One extreme role is the Rebellious Troublemaker, who often becomes angrily defiant and fights back against the rules and unrealistic expectations of the Bully, "Who cares! Screw it! Since I can't be perfect, I'll really mess up! Ha! You think you can control me! Just try!" Rebellious Troublemakers also rebel against other people who try to impose rules or control over you.

As the name suggests, the Rebellious Troublemakers will eat to rebel, "You think you can stop me from eating? Hah! I'll eat even more! Just try to stop me!" Usually the Rebellious Troublemakers will reach for the exact food the Bullies say is forbidden.

Another extreme role is the Numbing Troublemaker, the one who deadens intense feelings stirred up by the Bullies or the Exiles: "You can't stand these feelings. I can make them all go away." Numbing Troublemakers can trap us in endless pessimism, apathy, and procrastination, "Why bother? Why even try? It won't make any difference anyway."

When your emotions run high, Numbing Troublemakers will mindlessly eat anything to numb feelings. When you start to eat, you might feel as if you've stepped into a different zone: "It's like a wave just washes over me and, before I know it, the food is gone. I'm not aware in the moment I've eaten it."

Guess what happens next? The Bullies jump in and berate you for eating. The Exiles feel even more anxious and worthless. The Rebellious Troublemakers get angry and the Numbing Troublemakers convince you to eat even more. That's when the other extreme role kicks in: the Distracting Troublemaker.

When the other Parts escalate, the Distracting Troublemakers divert your attention away from what is going on to something urgent but unimportant. "Oh my! How many calories have I eaten today? I better get out my calculator." Without even realizing it, you stop dealing with the original problem that started the cycle in the first place and begin thinking about food or planning your next diet.

When extreme, the Parts are rigid and inflexible. They cling stubbornly to the same behaviors and refuse to try anything new, even if what they are doing isn't working and making it worse.

Breaking the Cycle

Establishing a firm sense of Self and getting the Parts back in balance and harmony is the goal of recovery. The process can last a long time. You will probably get frustrated many times along the way. You may lose motivation and want to give up.

I urge you to seek out a therapist even though a Part may say you should be able to recover without help, absolutely on your own. Recovery will be difficult even with a therapist; it would be almost impossible without. Without a therapist to act as a mediator and guide, your Parts may become even more extreme. A therapist can keep you motivated and moving forward, guide you in new directions, and point out patterns you are not even aware of. A therapist can create a safe place to try new ways of relating to yourself and to others. If your therapist is willing, you could read this book together.

In Chapter 3 we'll discuss how your Self might have been sacrificed and what to do to reclaim your Wise One Within.

Questions to Enhance Your Personal Recovery

Find a quiet time and some privacy to ponder the following questions. You may want to journal what you learn about yourself. I encourage you to share your answers with your therapist.

1   When reading this chapter, did you notice different Parts that popped up for you? Young, old, ageless? Male, female, both, neither? Loud, quiet? Submissive, aggressive?
2   Did you notice any Parts that reacted to you reading about Parts and Self? Describe the various Parts and their reactions.
3   Can you remember having glimpses of being in Self-energy? Try to recall times when you felt Compassionate, Curious, Clarity, Confident, or any of the other C qualities of Self.
4   Can you think of examples in your life when you have felt your Mentors, Advocates, and Kids? List some of these examples.
5   Think about times when you felt your Parts were out of balance. Give some examples of how you experienced the Bullies, Troublemakers, and Exiles.

3   What Happened? Why Me?

So what went wrong? What happened to your Self? As I said in Chapter 1, at some point in your life, consciously or unconsciously, your Self was sacrificed in some way.

Examining Your Past

In order to figure out how your Self was sacrificed, you need to look at your past. The examples in this chapter may be more extreme than your experiences and may bring up a lot of uncomfortable feelings that you have attempted to push down.

For example, my client Aviva believed that acknowledging how she felt – even in therapy – somehow violated a cultural taboo.

> My religion stresses honoring my mother and my father. When I think about how cruelly I was treated as a child, I feel like I am a bad person for not honoring them. Then that justifies what they did because, well, I must have deserved it. It's believed that abuse doesn't happen in my people, but then again, it's also believed my people don't get eating disorders and hey, I've got that too.

There is a lot to be learned when we allow ourselves to explore these difficult feelings and core beliefs. This information is explored solely to help you make sense of your situation, not to blame or point fingers. Blame is not productive; it keeps you caught in helplessness. Making sense of why and how you lost your connection to your Self can be empowering and motivating; this information can point out which Parts are stuck in negative patterns and need to change. As I tell my clients, "You can't change a pattern you are not aware of."

Critical Bullies may calm down when they realize your feelings and behaviors make sense and were, at one time, adaptive and evolved over time in response to the situation. Isolated Exiles may feel less alone when they realize others had similar situations and feel the same way they do, deep inside.

Gina experienced relief when she was finally able to admit what went on in her family.

> I can't tell anyone what happened in my family. My friends have great relationships with their mothers, but my mother is a tyrant. If I even hint at things my mother said or did, my friends look at me strange, 'What is wrong with you that you can't get along with your own mother?' It makes me feel so isolated. I feel better knowing I am not alone, that others have lived this too.

No one knows exactly what causes eating disorders. There are many theories being thrown around. My theory is that an eating disorder is how you learned to cope with the internal chaos that is the result of the sacrifice of your Self. There are two elements that led to your Self being sacrificed. The first one – pardon the psychobabble – is personal invalidation. The second is having a sensitive nature.

Personal Invalidation

When you were younger you received direct or indirect messages that told you it was not OK or not safe to be who you are. "Don't talk how you talk." "Don't act how you act." "Don't look how you look." "Don't feel how you feel." "Don't think how you think." "Don't be how you are." "Don't be who you are." "Just don't be you!"

These messages may have come from your culture and society, your family and friends, your religion, or the images and messages from television, movies, magazines and the internet.

For some, you may know exactly when you were invalidated. As I said previously, more than half of you are survivors of capital T Trauma: physical abuse, sexual abuse, or sexual assault. It's surprising how many of my clients have suffered or witnessed natural disasters, kidnapping, murder, and other violent crimes. You learned at an early age it wasn't safe to be in your body or in your Self.

Erin was the youngest of a large family where violence and drug and alcohol abuse were everyday occurrences. Her mother's attention was spread so thin that she had none left for Erin. Erin was rewarded for being "the good child" and she sacrificed all the Parts of herself that wanted or needed anything from her mother.

When Erin's father started showing special affection for her, she thought she was finally going to be loved and taken care of. Unfortunately, when Erin was 5 years old, her father began sexually abusing her. She craved his affection and attention, while also hating what was happening. Only by leaving her body was she able to resolve this conflict within. Erin was 13 when she stopped eating, literally starving away her Self.

Another example of Trauma can be found in the story of Gabriela, whose mother became pregnant with her from an affair. From the time she was little, Gabriela was repeatedly beaten and told, "You ruined my life! You should never have been born!" Whenever anything went wrong her mother would blame Gabriela. "If I didn't have you, I wouldn't have to spend so much money on food. I'd be able to buy nice things for myself."

Deep inside Gabriela believed "I am a burden to everyone. I have to take care of others or they will reject me." She was unable to ask for help of any kind and she couldn't trust that others would be there for her. In order to keep up the façade of strength, Gabriela binged and purged to numb out any and all wants and needs.

Now some of you may be thinking, "I wasn't beaten as a kid; I wasn't sexually abused. Nothing traumatic happened to me. So why did I get an eating disorder?"

Well, there's another kind of trauma that therapists call little t trauma. If Trauma is a stick of dynamite that blows a rock apart, trauma is the chip, chip, chip of a chisel on your self-esteem over time. It is subtle but continuous: being ignored or neglected, being bullied or ridiculed, experiencing humiliation or shame, feeling not cared for, being exposed to constant arguing or criticism, witnessing violence, or not being able to please someone. When you are exposed to these little t traumas over time, you begin to believe that these are "normal" experiences. Because little t trauma can be so varied, I will be giving a lot of examples.

Verbal Criticism

As a child, Angela often heard from her father, "No one loves a fat girl." She began to accept the statement as fact, so you can imagine how crucial thinness felt to her.

Ironically Angela's father battled his weight most of his adult life. I'm sure that if we asked Angela's father what he was trying to do for his daughter, he would say, "I love her and I want her to be happy. If she watches what she eats, maybe she won't end up like me. I want her to find a husband who will take care of her. If she's fat, I'm afraid that men will reject her and hurt her." But that's not how Angela internalized it: "I cannot please my father. I am too fat. I'm just not lovable."

Cultural Invalidation

Readers of color may identify with Aisha, an African American woman who grew up in a large family on the south side of Chicago. "When I was young, my family and friends used to tease me because my skin was so dark, darker than any of my siblings. My hair wasn't the 'good' kind.

When I read magazines or watched TV and movies, I never saw anyone who looked like me. I felt ugly; I hated the way I looked."

When Aisha went to college, she tried to fit in by dieting along with the white girls in her dorm. After losing a lot of weight, she found herself bingeing and purging to keep it off. When she turned to her sisters for help, they invalidated her again, "You don't have an eating disorder! That's a white girl disease! What are you trying to do? Be white?!"

Similarly, male clients often feel invalidated when they are told that only females get eating disorders.

Feeling Unimportant

Deanna always felt disconnected from her family.

> No one in my family cared about one another. No one ever stood up for each other. I never felt like anyone had my back, I was completely on my own. I felt so unimportant, like I wasn't even there. I yearned for connection with my family. It was only when my eating disorder got so bad that my doctor threatened to hospitalize me did my family notice, worry and step in to take care of me.

As you can imagine, recovery feels really scary to Deanna. "If I recover then they'll go back to the way they were. Then I'll never get what I want, a feeling of connection, of belonging. If I stay sick, I might get that, though at a price. If I recover, I lose them, but I gain my Self."

No-Win Situations

Maybe like Gina you tried hard to please an unpleasable person. No matter what Gina did, her mother screamed at her about it. On a visit home, she drove her mother to the mall. Trying to accommodate her mother, whose arthritis made it painful to walk, Gina offered to drop her off at the door before parking the car. Her mother was insulted that Gina didn't think she could walk from the car to the mall. So Gina parked the car. While they walked to the mall, her mother complained the whole way that she was in a lot of pain. She kept muttering loudly, "I'm suffering and no one cares about me at all!"

Gina's Kid Part, who had been experiencing these no-win situations for years, blamed herself,

> I just feel wrong inside. Whatever I feel is wrong, everything I do is wrong. I am wrong. After scooping out all the wrongness, whatever is left in there crumbles. That's when doubt comes in; no matter what's left inside I doubt that it's right. After hearing all the criticism I just can't be right. The doubt further destroys everything I have inside.

Early Medical Procedures

Brenda was the youngest in a large loving family. She was born with a bone disease that required frequent surgeries starting at the age of 2.

> I remember as a young child, the doctors would do things to my body that hurt, I didn't have a choice. The surgeries didn't work and they would have to do it all over again. My body didn't feel like it was in my control; I felt like there was something wrong with me deep inside, like I was doing something wrong or bad!

Because Brenda often had casts and was confined to a wheelchair she felt left out,

> My family was so afraid that I would hurt myself and have to go back to the hospital that they treated me like I was fragile. I wasn't allowed to play with the other children; I wasn't allowed to run, or jump rope, I've never learned to ride a bike! I always felt left out, like I don't fit in. My body just felt wrong!

Unspoken Rejection

Monica grew up in a good, loving family in an affluent suburb of Chicago. When she was a little girl, she and her mother looked through bridal magazines and planned elaborate weddings for Monica. Her mother pushed her into beauty contests and ballet lessons. But Monica liked to play softball and wear overalls. Her mother constantly yelled at her, "You look so ugly! You'll never get married if you keep dressing like a boy!"

Monica felt like a doll that her mother liked to dress up and place on a shelf for all to admire. To get affection and approval from her mother, Monica knew she had to be her mother's dress-up doll.

In junior high school, Monica realized she was a lesbian; she knew deep in her gut she was not who her mother wanted her to be and that Monica would be rejected if she came out. To continue to please her mother, Monica dated boys and wore frilly, feminine dresses to school dances. Inside, she felt she was living a lie, but dieting and bingeing and purging helped Monica avoid her inner emptiness.

In college, Monica had her first lesbian relationship – finally feeling she could be who she was meant to be inside. Her eating disorder symptoms stopped; she no longer felt the need to binge and purge. But every time she went home, Monica lived the lie again, and the bingeing and purging resumed.

Internal and External Invalidation

Dylan is a female-to-male transgender client whose personal invalidation started very early in his life.

I felt betrayed by my body as early as I can remember. As a young child I felt confused because people told me I was a girl, that my body was a girl, but deep inside I knew I was a boy. I didn't know what was wrong with me, but I felt completely alienated from what was going on in my body. My body on the outside just didn't match who I was on the inside.

In junior high, my body developed curves and I got my first period. I was horrified that this was happening and I couldn't do anything about it. I don't really remember what made me first stop eating, but I loved that my curves went away and my periods stopped!

When Dylan started college he met others who were transgender,

I was from a small town and had never heard of this before. I learned all I could about the process and when I came home for spring break I came out to my parents. At first they were shocked and confused. Eventually they told me they loved me, and asked how they could support and help me. I've started hormone therapy and my family has been great as my body and my appearance changes.

While Dylan is lucky to have such a validating family, he often finds that being in public feels the opposite.

When I meet people for the first time, I am often asked about my genitalia and my sex life! It's so intrusive! It's none of their business! People have told me that who I am doesn't exist, that what I'm doing is wrong! When I walk down the street, complete strangers make rude statements to me! I've even been spit on! Who does that to another person!

Core Belief System

From these shaming and invalidating messages, our Kid Parts develop what I call our core belief system: the internalized messages from our families, culture, and society. These messages eventually define who we think we are: "I am not OK," "I am not good enough," "I am not lovable as I am," "I shouldn't be me." I picture it as a ball of rubber bands – the beliefs in the center core being the most deeply embedded. Each message that is added to the core belief system reinforces the ones deep inside.

Young children believe everything that happens is a direct result of something they did. A child does not have the maturity to think, "Gee, no matter what I do, Daddy doesn't seem to be very happy. Poor Daddy must not be a very happy person on the inside." Instead she thinks, "Daddy's not happy. If I were a good girl, Daddy would be happy. Nothing I do is good enough. I'm bad."

So, as a child, every time you heard, "Don't be such a baby! You're just making a big deal out of nothing!" you tried to get rid of the Parts of you who were upset. You tried to deny how you were feeling, you attempted to silence your voice, and you scooped out another chunk of your Self.

The problem is that denying your feelings, silencing your voice, and scooping out chunks of your Self did nothing to truly change the situation. You were doomed to repeatedly sacrifice your Self to make Daddy happy, only to feel like a failure when it didn't last. So, as a child you continued to search for ways to change, to fix the problem; you sought something to hold on to, which gave you a sense of control.

Eventually, after scooping out so many chunks of yourself, you became hollowed out and empty; all that's left of you is a shell. Without your Self in a leadership role, like the junior-high band without a teacher, your Parts became chaotic, rebellious, anxious, and uncooperative.

Gradually you cut yourself off from your body where painful emotions and dangerous memories reside. Many clients have told me, "I feel as if I am just a head. My body is just a thing that I drag along with me. If I could get rid of my body entirely I would."

Your Sensitive Nature

At this point you may be wondering, "So why me? Why did I get an eating disorder? My trauma wasn't that bad! Others had it worse! What's wrong with me?!" So far in this chapter we've explored personal invalidation from one's environment. But there is an internal factor as well: most people with eating disorders have a sensitive nature. This is the second element that contributes to the sacrifice of Self.

Just hearing the word "sensitive" may feel like a kick in the gut. Sensitivity is often seen as a very negative trait, as if all of our reactions to situations are hugely overblown and incredibly inaccurate. Like Taylor says, "Dad's tantrums didn't seem to bother anyone else, like getting used to living next to a noisy airport. I always wondered why I couldn't. What was wrong with me?" (I find it interesting that she doesn't think, "What's wrong with him?")

Sensitivity is not a negative trait. Sensitive people are more empathic; they have the natural ability to know what other people are feeling and to walk in that person's shoes. Our sensitivity gives us genuine warmth and caring when dealing with others. I believe, in primitive societies, an empathic person with sensitive intuition would have been respected as a shaman or venerated as a sage. We make great ambassadors, diplomats, ministers, artists, and other professions that require these skills; my sensitivity is what makes me a natural as a psychotherapist.

Advocating

Because of our sensitivity, we often are outspoken and have a very strong sense of justice. These qualities are often not welcome in our families, like in *The Emperor's New Clothes*: The Emperor and his subjects are tricked into pretending that he is wearing "clothing so fine that only a fool could not see them." It took the wisdom of a child, an outspoken perceptive child, to point out "The Emperor has no clothes!" and the sham came tumbling down.

I ask my clients to imagine the Emperor's reaction to the child's remark. Do you think he said, "Thank you my child for exposing the sham?" I doubt it. I'm sure that he would have preferred the child to keep her mouth shut and save him from public humiliation.

If, as a child, you noticed things that your family didn't want to acknowledge, or asked questions your family didn't want to look at, your perceptions were invalidated, "Oh don't be silly. Daddy's just tired. He just had a hard day." Scoop! There goes another chunk of your Self.

Sensing Danger

In addition, sensitive people have a special ability to sense danger. If we look at any group (flamingos, squirrels, zebras, humans) a few are more sensitive than the rest. Imagine a herd of zebras grazing in a field. The sensitive zebras can detect subtle signs of movement and will alert the rest of the herd to run away from danger.

What would happen if all of the zebras were sensitive? The movement of one zebra would start a stampede. Conversely, if none of the zebras were sensitive, a lion would be able to walk right up to the herd and attack them without anyone noticing.

Because we are sensitive, we have the ability to protect our "herd." Because we are intuitive, empathic, and sensitive to other's feelings, we pick up subtle signs, clues, and nuances in others' body language or facial expressions. We read other people and take the temperature of the mood of the room. But, unlike zebras who always want to be alerted to danger, our families may have wanted to ignore difficulties and deny that problems exist, "Don't rock the boat!"

Our sensitivity "radar" helped us survive an inconsistent, chaotic, volatile or dangerous environment. Here's Taylor's experience:

> When my brother and I came home from school, before I even walked through the door I could sense, like electricity in the air, if my father was angry. My brother was oblivious and would bound right in. Dad inevitably started screaming at him for slamming the door too loudly, for whatever, for anything! Whereas I tried to slip in

and out unobserved. Most of the time it didn't work, he was already too upset. But if I was home first, I would know to be extra kind and caring to Dad. Sometimes it worked and I could disarm whatever was going on before he exploded.

Sensitivity + Invalidation

So, the combination of a sensitive nature and an invalidating environment caused the conflict within you. If you were sensitive and the environment was validating, there would be no problem. Imagine being raised by Mr Rogers, the wonderfully caring host of the kid's show on PBS. When something upset you, he would respond in his nurturing calming voice, "You're special just for being you. People can like you just the way you are. Bad things sometimes happen to good people."

Conversely, if you were insensitive in an invalidating environment, you may not have noticed and you could let it roll off your back. Less sensitive siblings may not have "felt" the problems as intensely. (Although don't assume they didn't. Even siblings who seem to have their act together can be hurting inside; they just do not turn to food to cope.)

Sensitive Parts Disowned

Our feelings were often invalidated because others did not feel as sensitively as we did: "There's nothing to be afraid of. Don't be such a scaredy-cat. You're just being a cry-baby. You're just too sensitive." After repeatedly being shamed and told we shouldn't feel what we were feeling, we created a core belief, "I'm too sensitive! I shouldn't feel this way. There's something wrong with me." When we disowned the Parts of us that were scared or cried, these Parts became Exiles.

Understanding the Exiles

After having your feelings and reactions invalidated over and over, year after year, you become out of touch with your Self and lose the voice of wisdom within. Even when you react accurately to a situation, Exiles doubt that you could possibly be right. The more the Exiles doubt your reaction, the less you trust your own inner wisdom.

The Exiles become dependent upon what other people tell you you "should" be feeling, thinking, doing, acting, behaving, speaking, and so forth. Self-doubt makes you vulnerable to invalidating messages from the media: "You'll be popular and have lots of friends if you are skinny and drink Diet Peppy and wear Clever Girl mascara!"

We've been brought up to be good little girls and boys; good little children never speak up, never get angry, and are pretty and cute. Good little children are always nice and do what others want. Good little children never say, "No, I don't want to hug Aunt Maybelle; she makes me feel icky inside!" Oh no! If we speak up, others won't like it; we might make others mad and then they won't like us, which reinforces our negative core beliefs.

As good little children we never developed the skills, resources, and tools necessary to cope with what life dishes out. Without a voice and a choice, we were powerless. We swallowed our voice, sacrificed our Self, and gave Aunt Maybelle a hug because that's what good little children do. We were at the mercy of the whims of others. Life felt like a very dangerous and out-of-control place.

Exiles Feel Shame

The Exiles believe they are unlovable, unlikable, and unworthy inside; they feel shame and try to hide these feelings from others. Exiles live in fear that others will find out the "truth:" "I can't let people get to know me. If they ever found out how needy I really am, they'd be disgusted and reject me." Pulling away from other people causes isolation and loneliness, which just reinforces the negative core beliefs of the Exiles.

Bullies Overcompensate

Our Bully steps in to keep our sensitive Exiles in check: "What's wrong with you! You are such a baby! Stop making such a big deal out of nothing! No one else is bothered by this. Quit complaining!"

The Bully also tries to overcompensate for feeling worthless by setting extremely perfectionistic standards. Because no one can consistently meet such high standards, the Bully criticizes and yells, which reinforces the Exiles feeling like failures.

Troublemakers Step in

Not being able to stand the anxiety and tension that builds up, a Troublemaker steps in: "I can't stand it anymore! Food! I need to eat!"

The pattern starts all over again: The Exiles feel shame about eating, Bullies continue to criticize, which just brings us back to the Troublemakers again. The pattern gets more entrenched each time it is repeated.

Find Your Wise Self

Let's go back to the example of the junior-high-school band whose teacher didn't show up. Imagine and feel the chaos, anarchy, and noise once again. Now visualize a kind, compassionate, benevolent but firm teacher steps into the room. What do you imagine now? Most people say they hear a hush and the noise stops. The band members stop fighting and get back into their proper seats. Order is restored. The teacher smiles at them and picks up her baton and the band starts to play in harmony and cooperatively once again.

The same is true of our Parts. The key to all of this is to get the teacher back in the junior-high-school band, to find your Self, or the voice of wisdom within. Then, and only then, will the Bullies calm down and become Mentors, the Exiles will be healed and become playful Kids, and the Troublemakers will be free to establish balance and self-care as the Advocates. In Chapter 4, you will learn ways to find your sense of Self.

Questions to Enhance Your Personal Recovery

Find a quiet time and some privacy to ponder the following questions. You may want to journal what you learn about yourself. I encourage you to share your answers with your therapist.

1   When reading this chapter, did you notice different Parts that popped up for you? Young, old, ageless? Male, female, both, neither? Loud, quiet? Submissive, aggressive?
2   Can you think of some of the core beliefs you developed from the messages you received from people in your past?
3   Which of the examples in this chapter resonated with you or reminded you of your environment, culture, family?
4   Can you think of times when you sacrificed your Self or a Part of yourself? To whom or for what did you sacrifice it?
5   What are some examples of your Exile feeling shame or doubt? Anxiety or fear? Self-blame?
6   How does your Bully overcompensate? What situations make your Bully set extremely high standards?
7   How do your Troublemakers react to the Exile or Bully?

Reference

Andersen, Hans Christian (1959) *The Emperor's New Clothes*. New York, NY: Oxford University Press

4   Finding Your Self

OK, it's time to find your Self and start forming new relationships with your Parts. In order to recover, you need to put your Self back in charge of your Parts, like getting the teacher to step back into the junior-high band room and stay there.

Insight does not automatically lead to a change in behavior. Your eating disorder will not just automatically go away. So it's time to do something different. You have to make your recovery a conscious decision each day. As I often say to my clients, "If you always do what you've always done, you'll always get what you've always gotten."

Inner Emptiness

Almost without exception, when a client doesn't feel a sense of Self, she describes an inner emptiness, a frightening sense that something vital is missing deep inside. Here's what it is like for Michelle: "I just feel like Swiss cheese inside; there are all these holes. It makes me anxious to feel them. I tried to fill the holes by eating. It works for a moment, but it doesn't fill the holes for long."

The emptiness is the potential where your Self will be. If you want to plant a rose bush, you need to dig a hole so there is a place for it. The emptiness inside is where you will experience your Self again. We're going to bring your Self out of hiding and put it back in charge. Just as the hole disappears when you place the rose bush in it, the inner emptiness will disappear when you find your Self; you will feel fulfilled, full and filled again.

Hidden Self

Your Self is there. It may be hidden away for safekeeping under layers of defenses and old issues, but it's there. As I mentioned in the last chapter, at some point you learned that it was not OK for you to be you. Some of you remember feeling good about yourself until puberty, and others say they felt bad even before they entered pre-school.

Many clients talk about their early teens as being the most painful time of their lives, like Michelle:

> In third or fourth grade, I felt really confident. I liked myself a lot. I was comfortable in my body. I remember having eating contests. Who could eat the most? Standing up on the table cheering because I won the eating contest. And it wasn't a binge! Oh no! I would eat and just forget about it.

Michelle continues tearfully, "I lost her in junior-high school. I wonder where that person is. Where did she go?"

Without a sense of Self, your Parts became chaotic, noisy, uncooperative, rebellious, anxious – just like the members of the junior-high band when the teacher stopped showing up. Depending on how long your Parts have been like this, they may be very suspicious of any change to this system. If your Self has been absent for a long time, your Parts may need time to trust that your Self will not leave them again. Some of the Parts may feel relieved that the Self is coming back, but other Parts, especially the one who took over as the Pseudo-Self, may feel threatened and try to sabotage your recovery efforts.

As your Parts feel heard, appreciated, and taken care of, they will calm down and allow more of your Self to emerge. As the trust builds up, your Parts will begin to reorganize around a healthier Self-led system.

Getting Familiar with Self

As you recover your sense of Self, it may feel familiar. Some of you may already have glimpses of Self from time to time. You might remember when you knew something was right – not a thinking kind of knowing – but a deep-in-your-gut kind of knowing. And even if others disagreed, you knew that it was right for you.

Ruth described an experience of knowing something from deep within:

> A while ago I went with my boyfriend to a party at his office. He was really nervous and acting strange. He kept going into other rooms, just leaving me sitting there all alone.
>
> A Critical Part of me kept screaming, 'You're so fat he can't stand to be seen with you! You are such a loser he's embarrassed to be with you.'
>
> I could hear the Critic, but deep inside I felt something, not a voice but just a sense that the Critic was wrong. I just knew it wasn't because of me.
>
> Later on I found out he was cheating on me and his coworkers knew. Somehow, deep inside, I just knew our relationship was in trouble. Maybe the Critic was trying to prevent me from feeling betrayed and hurt.

Some of you may be thinking, "Yeah, right. Everyone else who reads this book has a Self hidden away, but not me. I'm defective, I'm hopeless." This is probably a Skeptical Bully who is trying to protect you from being hurt or disappointed. In this and the next three chapters you will learn ways to calm even the most skeptical of Parts.

Recognizing Your Self

Your Self is physically *subtle* and verbally very quiet – while your Parts have become physically **INTENSE** and verbally **LOUD!**

Your Self may be easily out-shouted by aggressive and forceful Parts. As you know, "The squeaky wheel gets the grease," so you gave your attention to the Parts who were the loudest. As you make your way back to your Self, the clamoring will become quieter and the Parts will become more cooperative.

The Self is usually experienced deep in the body, as inner wisdom or gut intuition, as unconditional positive self-acceptance and regard. When in Self-energy you feel calm, peaceful, content, and without worry; you know what is right for you, even when it is not the easy or popular thing to do. It is a deep-seated sense of inner strength and wisdom within. When you are in your Self, you know that no matter what happens you can handle it; you have all the resources you need within you. From this strength and knowledge you feel calmly confident and in charge of your life.

The goal is to live your life with your Self in charge as much as possible. When life throws you a zinger – and it will, not because you are weak or defective, but because you are a human living in a real and uncontrollable world – your Parts will react and need help. The Self will notice and compassionately attend to their needs. Once the problem has been taken care of, the Parts and Self can then return to their healthy new system within.

Once you know what it feels like to be in Self-energy, you will be able to consciously "breathe into" that feeling. At first it will feel strange, but the more you practice, the more comfortable and familiar it will feel. Amanda described it well: "It's like trying to remember a song I've heard only once. But after I hear it again I remember it. And if I hear it again and again, over time I can sing it to myself whenever I want."

Exercises to Find Self

I have included several exercises to help you find your Self. Try each one several times. Repeat the exercises as you go on to the next three chapters. When you work with your Parts, they will calm down and your sense of Self will strengthen too.

Each of these exercises will take practice. A Perfectionistic Part may say, "You tried it once and it didn't work. It only lasted like five minutes.

You're such a failure!" But if you think about it; it did work even if only for five minutes. The next time you try it, it might last 25 minutes, then two hours. Eventually it will last a day and a half before you have to do it again.

As you read through the exercises, feel free to combine pieces of each of the exercises to suit your needs. Scented candles or incense and soft meditative music can enhance the experience. It may be useful to ask a close friend or your therapist to make a recording of the exercises. Clients have found it helpful to listen to my CD *Imagine Being at Peace:* ✗ *A Guided Imagery Meditation*, which guides you through a deep-body relaxation using calm-colored breathing.

1. Using the C Qualities of Self

In this first exercise you are going to use your breath to create a space within and invite the qualities of Self to enter the space.

- Sit back, relax as best you can, close your eyes.
- Imagine calmness has a color and slowly inhale a calm-colored breath. Notice the movement of the air entering your nose, your throat, your chest, and finally down to your diaphragm.
- Now exhale slowly and notice the movement of the air leaving your diaphragm, your chest, your throat, and finally your nose.
- With each calm-colored breath, imagine that you are inflating an empty space, like a bubble, inside and around your body. Each calm-colored breath pushes out all thoughts, emotions, and sensations from the space. When you exhale, visualize all your thoughts, emotions, and sensations leaving your body and mind.
- When your mind and body feel full of the calm-color, ask each of the C qualities of Self to enter the space one at a time. Concentrate on each one for two or three calm-colored breaths.
- Step back from yourself and, using your Capacity for objectivity imagine that you can watch yourself like an actor on a movie screen.
- Allow yourself to become Curious: "I wonder what this exercise will be like?"
- Ground yourself and your body in the present moment and be Current.
- Notice that your body and mind feel Centered and Calm.
- Remember what it feels like to experience Courage and Confidence.
- Feel the warmth of loving Compassion.
- Notice that your situation seems to gain Clarity.
- Use Creativity to see new solutions for your situation.
- Finally, feel a Connection between your Self and your Parts, between yourself and people in your life, and between yourself and something greater – or the bigger picture of Life.

2. Ask Your Parts to Step Aside

If your Parts are not allowing you to breathe into Self-energy, or if your Self is critical or condemning, then a Part, most likely a Bully, is trying to take over. (Even though the words "critical" and "condemning" begin with the letter C, these are not qualities of the Self.) You will need to ask the Part to step aside in order to access your Wise One Within without interference.

In this exercise, I will name several Parts that most people meet when they do the exercise. But, as you do the exercise, allow your Parts to arise in whatever order they appear. I am going to use the female pronoun instead of the awkward he/she or him/her. Feel free to change the gender of the Parts if necessary to match your own experience.

This exercise can be done sitting in a comfortable position with both feet on the floor and eyes closed. Or it can be done as a walking meditation, walking slowly along a quiet path, in a circle in an open space or even in a labyrinth. If walking, keep your eyes with a soft focus, so that you are more attuned to your inner experience than outer images.

- Picture a pleasant path, a familiar sidewalk, a lovely trail in the woods, a beautiful carpet runner, a yellow brick road – whatever you see in your mind's eye is fine. The path slopes gently upward, far to the horizon. As you walk along the path see it as you would if you were actually walking on a path. If you look down you see just your legs and feet, rather than seeing your entire body as if on a movie screen.

- Breathe your calm-color deeply into your body with each step. Imagine the texture of the path under your feet. Feel the sun on your face. Maybe there is a gentle breeze.

- As you walk along the path, become aware of any thoughts, feelings, or body sensations that arise. For example, a Worried Part may be experienced as a feeling of uneasiness in your stomach, and the thought "Oh my! What if I'm doing this wrong?" Stop walking and take a deep calm-colored breath. Visualize the Worried Part as a person standing by the side of the path. With loving Compassion, tell the Worried Part, "Please wait here. I will be right back. I need to do this by myself." Make a comfortable and safe place for the Worried Part to wait; give her whatever she needs while she waits: a bench, a blanket, a pillow, a stuffed animal, even a foam bat or punching bag. Don't think about it too much; trust that your Self will just know what the Part needs.

- Start walking forward again, breathing the calm-color deeply, until you have another feeling, thought or sensation; maybe this time a Young Part feels scared, "Oh no! What's up ahead? Are we going to be all right?" Stop again and take a deep calm-colored breath. Turn to the Scared Part and warmly say, "I need to be by myself right now. I need you to wait here. And I will be right back." Again, give the Scared Part what it needs to be comfortable so you can go forward.

- Breathe the calm-color deeply again. Walk forward until you have another feeling, thought or sensation; maybe a clenching in your stomach and a tightness in your jaw, and the thought, "You are so pathetic! What a waste of time!" Again, stop walking and take a deep calm-colored breath. Calmly but firmly ask the Critical Part to step aside, "Please wait here. I will be right back. I need to do this by myself." Give the Critical Part what it needs to wait before you walk forward again.
- Keep repeating this with each feeling, thought, or sensation that arises. Breathe the calm-color deeply. Separate from each Part until you feel peaceful and alone in your Self. You notice your mind is quieter, Calmer; your body is much more grounded and Centered. You start to see things more Clearly, and maybe feel Courage, Confidence, and Compassion within your body. You may feel a Connection with the bigger picture of life, the energy of nature or a higher power.
- You are now standing at the horizon. Feel the sun warming your face and body. Feel the sun calming and healing your body and mind. Take in the beauty and magnificence of the view. Stay here a while, enjoying the pleasantness of the quiet and calmness. Cement these feelings within your body so that you know what it feels like and can recall it when you need it in the future. You are experiencing your Self; this is who you were meant to be.
- Turn around to leave the horizon; imagine returning back down the Path. Now that you are in your Self, the Parts see you as transformed. As you meet each Part, they recognize the Self within you and they calm down. Because you are seeing them through the Compassionate and loving eyes of the Wise One Within, they will appear different from when you left them.
- As your wise and loving Self, you can see each Part's positive role and can feel warmth, gratitude, and nurturance for all of them. There may be a feeling of cooperation among the Parts as you rejoin them. This is the beginning of a healthy change in your relationship with your Parts.[1]

3. Meeting the Wise One Within

Some of you may need to actually visualize your Self as a person – the Wise One – to feel your Self-energy. Even if you imagine a real person, such as your therapist or poet Maya Angelou, the feelings you evoke come from you, from your Self.

The goal is to eventually, with practice, be able to "conjure" up the Wise One Within by taking one calm-colored breath and stepping into the serene and loving wisdom that is always within you.

Your Wise One may be female, male, or gender neutral; but for simplicity's sake I am going to use the female pronoun again. Your Wise One may appear as a human, an animal, an object, or simply as a color, mist, or glow. Don't worry if you cannot see the Wise One's face. This is actually a positive sign of Self-energy: since you are looking at your Self from your Self, it may not be possible to see your own face.

This exercise can be done at the end of the Path Exercise or done on its own. Again, see it from your own eyes rather than seeing your whole body as if on a movie screen.

- Start by taking several calm-colored breaths and, when you are relaxed, imagine a very inviting house, residence or dwelling. Notice a feeling of welcome anticipation as you walk towards the house. Deep inside you know the Wise One Within lives there, and you know the Wise One is expecting you and wants to be with you.
- Go up to the door and knock. The door opens and the Wise One welcomes you. Notice what she looks like, what she is wearing, how she holds her body, what she is doing. If you cannot see the Wise One that is fine too; just feel her loving presence.
- Observe how you feel in her loving presence; give yourself permission to take in her warmth and care. Notice what it feels like to be with someone who has total unconditional positive acceptance and regard for you. Allow her Calmness and Wisdom to enter deep into your body; feel it within you. Reinforce that feeling inside your body so you can remember it later.
- Look around inside the house, notice the furniture, décor, or lighting; or notice the absence of furniture, décor, or lighting. She may offer you tea or something to eat; notice how you feel eating or drinking in her loving presence. Also notice the feeling of total unconditional positive acceptance and regard; it is also fine with her if you do not want to eat or drink what is offered.
- While you are with the Wise One, you sense she wants you to ask a question. Don't think about it; just allow a question to bubble up from deep within. Now listen for her answer; just accept it as it is, even if it does not make sense to you now.
- Then she reaches into a pocket and gives you a gift. If it is wrapped, go ahead and open it. Whatever she gives you, accept it, even if it doesn't make sense.

When it is time to go the Wise One looks you in the eyes and says, "Whenever you need me, I am always within you. I am just one breath away." As she hugs you, take a deep breath and feel her wisdom, warmth, and loving compassion deep within you. Any time you need her, all you need to do is take one deep breath, and her strength and guidance will always be within you. You can ask her anything, and the answers will come to you from within.

Afterwards I encourage you to find or purchase the gift from the Wise One. Put this object, or even a picture of the object, where you will see it often. Every time you see it, take a deep calm-colored breath and connect to the Wise One within.

4. Accessing Self through a Young Part

Another way to access your Self is through feeling Curiosity, Capacity for objectivity, and Compassion towards your Young Part. To begin, go find a picture of yourself at a very young age that I describe as: "When you look at her, you know she loves her Self, loves life, and expects the world to love her back." (Don't worry; I'll wait while you look for it.)

My clients have brought in the most incredible pictures. Joni, who you will meet in the next chapter, brought in this one (see Figure 4.1).

Look at this adorable little girl. Unselfconsciously she lifts up her arms and her shirt exposes her cute round belly. Looking at the smile on her face, you can't help but smile too. It may strike you, as it did for Joni, that someone loved her or noticed her enough to take the picture.

If you do not have a picture of yourself at a young age, you can use one of a child you know and love. A picture from the internet will also work for this exercise.

Figure 4.1 Typical client picture of Young Part (printed with permission).

Do you have a photo? Good. If not, ask your Skeptic Part to allow you to try this exercise as an experiment. If the Skeptic Part won't step aside, just read through the exercise and try it later.

- Breathe your calm-color deeply and clear your mind of any thoughts or judgments. In the beginning of this exercise, step back and look at the picture objectively. Pretend this is any child, not you. You may start to feel amusement or laughter inside; that is perfectly OK.
- Notice what you are feeling towards the child in the photo. If you feel anger, hatred, disgust, sadness, or fear during this exercise, ask that Part to step aside like in the Path Exercise. Give the Part what she needs and reassure her that you will come back to her, but for now you need to stay in the C qualities of Self-energy. (If the Part will not step aside, try this exercise later.)
- Allow yourself to feel curiosity and wonder. Slowly scan your body and find where you experience curiosity. Discern this feeling from any other thought, emotion, or body sensation in that area of your body. Looking at the picture with curiosity, wonder what the child must be thinking and feeling about herself at the moment the picture was taken. Allow the child's thoughts and feelings of self-love and self-pride to emerge.
- Now view the child as yourself. (If you are looking at a picture of another child, imagine doing this exact act as a child. You may not have put a doll on your head, but I am positive you did something just as cute.) If your thoughts or feelings change from curiosity to anger, hatred, disgust, sadness, or fear, ask the Part to step aside. If the Part will not step aside, go back to viewing the child anonymously or try this exercise later.
- Remember or imagine what it felt like to feel good, to feel proud of yourself, to feel love towards yourself and the world. Allow feelings of love, warmth, or nurturance for yourself as a child to surface.
- See the child through the loving eyes of Compassion. Where in your body do you feel Compassion? What does Compassion want to do or say to the child? Allow words of nurturance to bubble up from within. Allow yourself to feel close and emotionally connected to the child.

Experiencing the Wise One Within: Marlene

Marlene describes finding her Wise One Within on her journey towards recovery from overeating:

Long ago I became aware of how much shame I carried. I decided to create the Perfect Mother for myself in my mind. I tried on many types of mothers until I found one that resonated with my heart and soul. Once the qualities I needed were clear to me – total acceptance, loving, reassuring, supportive, and embracing – I put this person into my consciousness. I told myself that every time a shame feeling came up, instead of reacting to it, I would let it be a red flag to bring my Perfect Mother to the forefront of my mind. In my mind's eye, she would hold me and tell me how wonderful I was just as I was. If my mind began to move into the negativity of shame I would hold onto the image of this Perfect Mother and just keep having her support me, love me, tell me over and over how great I was. Within six months of doing this every single time shame appeared, the shame was healed and has never returned.

Experiencing the Wise One Within: Patty

Let's hear how Patty used her loving Wise One Within to stop a downward spiral that usually would have led to a binge. Patty had a lot to do and was feeling stressed, anxious, and overwhelmed. She felt guilty that she couldn't do it all; like she was a disappointment to her family.

I suddenly stopped and took a deep breath to summon my Wise One. I asked her to be with me. Deep inside, I felt her loving presence. She told me that I was doing the best I could and that was just fine. I felt so much better after that and was able to get back on track. I didn't binge and got a lot accomplished.

Experiencing the Wise One Within: Elece

For years, Elece took care of everyone except herself. She and her business partner, Joe, owned a store together. While Joe took time off to play golf, Elece deciphered the orders he scribbled, filled in for any employee who was absent, traveled to trade shows, and designed new products. She also regularly drove Joe to and from their store, cleaned his apartment, and did his laundry. When Elece finally made it home at night, she was exhausted. The only way she relaxed was to binge or drink.

Elece often felt her life was out of her control. Deep inside she felt angry and resentful. She protected herself by withdrawing and isolating, but ended up feeling lonely, unloved, and not good enough.

Several of Elece's Parts were caught in a negative cycle. A Young Part felt worthless and unlovable while another Part was overly critical of everything she did. A third Part told her that she deserved to give herself a treat by eating and drinking as much as she wanted.

To change this cycle, Elece and I created a daily ritual to slow down her life and access her loving Wise One Within. Because Elece was so busy, her ritual had to be quick, simple, and easy. So we embellished what she already did in the morning, giving each of her Parts what they needed, all in less than three minutes.

Elece took a mug of coffee and sat in her favorite chair. Breathing her calming color, she repeated the Serenity Prayer aloud, "God, grant me the serenity to accept the things I cannot change, courage to change the things I can, and the wisdom to know the difference."

She imagined Young Elece sitting on her left side. Allowing compassion, empathy, and warmth to enter her heart she lovingly told Young Elece, "You are fun, creative and lovable, just as you are." Taking another deep calm-colored breath, she saw her Mentor on her right. Allowing appreciation to enter her heart, Elece thanked the Mentor for pushing her forward, for wanting her to have meaning and fulfillment in her life.

Taking another deep calm-colored breath, Elece pictured her Advocate sitting in front of her. Feeling grateful, Elece thanked the Advocate for finding balance in her life. She promised all her Parts that she would slow down and make decisions from the Wise One Within.

At the store, whenever she saw her calming color, which was the color of her business logo, Elece took a deep calming breath and repeated the Serenity Prayer. When she was in Self-energy, Elece made wise choices about the use of her personal time; she agreed to do only things that truly brought her pleasure and started saying no to many other requests. With her extra time and energy, she filled her evenings with activities that made her feel nurtured and taken care of.

Experiencing the Wise One Within: Jennifer

Similar to how Elece used the color of her business logo, Jennifer linked the sound of her cell phone to her Wise One Within. (You can use any common object: your keys, your computer, even trees, or stop signs.) First, Jennifer held her cell phone as she took deep calm-colored breaths and relaxed. With her eyes closed, Jennifer listened to the sound of her cell phone while, at the same time, she took a deep calm-colored breath and felt the Wise One's loving presence within her. Jennifer practiced taking a deep calm-colored breath before answering her cell phone and could take each call with the guidance and wisdom of her Self.

During the day, every time Jennifer heard a phone ring, she breathed into that calm place of peace within. She noticed that the more she connected with her Self, the calmer her Parts were throughout the day.

Experiencing the Wise One Within: Molly

When you slow down enough to hear what the Wise One Within has to say, sometimes you hear something that deep down you already knew but your Parts didn't want you to hear. Here's Molly's experience with finding her Self.

Molly was in a nine-year relationship with Sean, who had a very short fuse. He would scream at her at the least annoyance; he treated her badly, criticized, and humiliated her publicly. Her family pressured Molly to marry him anyway, "You're not getting any younger, you know."

Afraid of doing anything that might set him off, Molly became extremely passive and felt stuck in the relationship. Her Critical Part blamed her, "If you weren't such a loser, he would be nicer to you. It's all your fault. You're fat. You need to lose weight." A Young Vulnerable Part felt ashamed and worthless and doubted all of her thoughts, feelings, and reactions. By following a strict diet she was able to push these feelings away. But, several times a week, Molly woke up and found evidence that she had binged during the night.

During our sessions Molly could hear the Wise One Within and knew that she did not like how Sean treated her. But, when she was with Sean, her Parts "forgot" what she worked on in therapy.

Gradually, as her sense of Self became stronger, Molly began to speak up and disagree with him. Sean did not like Molly's new assertiveness. This was a very difficult time for her but, when she spoke up, her night bingeing decreased. By using her voice, she no longer needed to push her feelings down with food.

Eventually, Sean broke off the relationship with Molly. She became aware of a deep wisdom within, "All was not as it seemed in the relationship." Molly's Wise One Within knew that the unhealthy things she did during their relationship were attempts to protect her from Sean's emotional abuse. During one session she said, "I have a feeling in my heart that I am OK. When I am with people who love me as I am, I can be my Self. I'm going to be fine."

Practice Being in Self

If your Parts have been in control – or, more accurately, out of control – for a long time, they will not just magically pop into healthy roles. It's going to take practice, practice, practice, and more practice.

After a while you will notice that you are in your Self more than not. You will do, think, and say things that are calming, soothing, and compassionate to yourself and others. You will feel an inner harmony and cooperation with all your Parts. You will have discovered the person you were meant to be.

When you are in Self-energy, the inner emptiness will begin to be filled, and you and your Parts will stop feeling alone. Inwardly you feel connected to your Parts and your Parts feel connected to you. Gina said, "I used to feel alone in a crowd of people. Now I feel fine even when I am by myself."

You may also feel a spiritual connection with something greater than yourself, where you fit in the bigger picture of life. Some clients feel closer to the energy of nature or a tie to all of humankind. Many clients feel closer to a higher power as they perceive it; some feel God's presence.

Erin puts it profoundly, "Recovery led me to my Self. My Self led me to God. God led me to other people. My Self couldn't be the last stop."

In Chapter 5, we will begin to change your relationship with your Bullies.

Questions to Enhance Your Personal Recovery

Find a quiet time and some privacy to ponder the following questions. You may want to journal what you learn about yourself. I encourage you to share your answers with your therapist.

1   When reading this chapter, did any Parts pop up for you? How were you able to ask them to step aside and allow you to get back into Self-energy?
2   Reflect for a moment on what these meditative exercises were like for you. Did you notice your Self-energy taking center? Did your Parts get louder or quieter? Which feelings did you experience?
3   What qualities of Self do you most easily identify with? What quality is hardest?
4   What Parts did you meet during the Path Exercise? What helped them to step aside? What did they need from you in order to wait?
5   Describe your first experience of meeting your Wise One Within. What did the house look like outside and in? If you could see the Wise One describe her or him. What question did you ask? What gift did you receive? Can you determine the significance of the gift?
6   What are some ways – using a color or an object – that can help you design a ritual to practice getting into Self-energy?

Note

1 Thank you to Richard C. Schwartz PhD for permission to use the Path Exercise that he developed. This exercise is on his CD *Meditations for Self* that is available at: http://www.selfleadership.org/ifs-store.html

Reference

Grabowski, A. (2005) *Imagine Being at Peace: A Guided Imagery Meditation CD*

5 Making Peace with the Bully

> I can't stand it anymore! There's a Bully in my head who yells at everything I do! I can't even comb my hair without being condemned for how pathetic I am. If I make a single mistake she calls me a loser or a failure! I hate her so much! I know you've told me that we don't get rid of our Parts, but I would love it if I could! All she does is make me feel worthless and inadequate.
>
> Stacey

I am sure you can identify with Stacey's complaint. I know I can. When I described The Self to you, I had to give a lengthy explanation. But, with just one example of the Bully, you know exactly what I mean.

Qualities of the Bully

The Bully – also known as the Critic or the Judge – is usually very verbal, loud, abusive, punitive, and shaming. The Bully uses humiliation and name-calling; she swears even if you normally don't:

> Oh my God! What the #$%* is wrong with you! What a loser! You are completely hopeless! You don't even deserve this job! I don't know why your boss puts up with you. If they knew the real you, none of your coworkers would ever talk to you again. If you weren't so fat, this would never have happened. You can't eat today!

I'm sure you can fill in the rest.

The Bully's Thinking Patterns

The Bully is trapped in distorted, perfectionistic, and black-or-white thinking:

- If you're not perfect, you are a FAILURE!
- If you made a mistake, you are a complete LOSER!

- If one person doesn't like you, then everybody HATES you!
- If you are not flawless, then you are WORTHLESS!

In the Bully's eyes you don't make mistakes, you are a mistake. You didn't fail, you are a failure. She also blames your mistakes on your eating or weight, even though there is no logical tie. The Bully offers no solutions to your problems.

However, the Bully has a positive intention for you, but it is buried beneath layers of shame and judgment. You may have to dig very deep to get to anything worth saving.

The Bully as the Pseudo-Self

The Bully is the Part that you may mistake for your Self. When the Self was sacrificed and was not available to take care of young vulnerable Exiles, the Bully took over this important job. In its own twisted logic, the Bully actually thinks its harsh and abusive tone is somehow protecting the young vulnerable Exiles.

But the Bully is not the Self and does not possess the C qualities of the Self. Often the Bully's "solutions" just make your problems worse. Here's how Erin describes her Bully, whom she experiences as male:

> Not only did my Bully berate me for each and every mistake I made, but he saved the memory of these and compiled them into a 'fact-based thesis' to prove my unworthiness: I was unworthy of love, kindness, generosity, care, concern, and any other shred of dignity that I might have used to lift myself out of bed each and every morning.

This so-called "fact-based thesis" reawakens and repeatedly reinforces the negative core beliefs held by the Exiles. The Exiles feel more and more hopeless, anxious, and worthless after each encounter with the Bully.

To make matters worse, the Bully never considers her role in this cycle. She projects all the blame outward. She is not the problem. You are. She is not responsible. You are. She has to talk to you this way because, deep inside, you are hopeless (or so she tells you).

Rethinking the Bully

Like the junior-high band missing its teacher, your Parts are stuck in negative patterns. As the Bully yells louder, and the Exiles feel worthless, the Troublemakers get involved, the Rebels act out, and the Numbing or Distracting Parts get busy. Then the Bully yells louder, the Exiles feel more worthless, the Troublemakers act up . . . Do-si-do, around you go, in a never-ending cycle.

Without the Self, the Bully and the other Parts keep repeating the same old arguments, "I have to yell because you don't listen to me." "Well I'm not going to listen to you because you yell at me."

They don't try anything different; they just repeat their arguments, getting more and more stuck, never resolving anything, "Why would I listen to you when you say the nastiest things?" "I say the nastiest things because you don't listen." This goes on and on forever.

If Bully Was "Gone"

Like Stacey, you might be wondering why do you even need the Bully? Well, imagine that I threw your Bully out the window and she was hit by a big truck. There. The Bully is gone. No more yelling. No more criticism. How do you feel?

Your first reaction is probably relief, "Great! I feel so much better. I feel lighter and freer!"

I'll let you enjoy the fantasy for a moment before I ask, "But what would go haywire if the Bully was completely gone forever? What if there was absolutely no self-criticism in your head ever again?"

You may have to think about this a while before you realize, "I probably wouldn't be a very nice person. I would say mean things without caring. I'd never achieve anything. I'd just lay on the couch all day in my robe and watch reality TV."

Balancing the Bully

This reminds me of something I learned in high-school biology. A long time ago, a town decided to get rid of all the wolves in the area. Soon after, rats and mice overran the town. By killing off the wolves, the checks and balances of the ecosystem were thrown off. A new problem developed.

Without an Inner Critic, the balance among your Parts would be thrown off and other extreme Parts would just take over. Without someone motivating you to do something productive with your life, your Numbing Part might take over. One day would blend into the next without a care. You would never grow or change or get any further in life.

At first, your Kid Parts may enjoy the freedom. You may imagine children jumping on the bed and eating jellybeans for breakfast. But, after a while, the Kids would realize no one is there to take care of them; they soon would feel alone, anxious, and helpless – and sick to their stomachs.

The Bully to Mentor Continuum

Each of your Parts is on a continuum (see Figure 5.1). At one end, the Part is balanced, functional, and healthy (this is represented by a circle). I call this Part the Mentor. At the other end – when the Part is extreme, dysfunctional, and unhealthy – I call her the Bully.

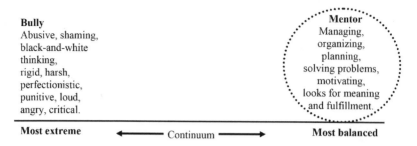

Figure 5.1 Bully to Mentor Continuum.

Qualities of the Mentor

The Mentor wants to motivate you, to push you to learn, grow, and move forward in your life. The Mentor helps you to live your life with integrity and values. In the long run, her goal is for you to be the best you can be, to find fulfillment and meaning in your life.

In addition, the Mentor manages your day-to-day life: pays bills, organizes schedules, plans social events, manages multiple deadlines, figures out finances, and juggles the upkeep of your car, house, possessions, and your health and body. The list goes on and on.

The Mentor speaks in a respectful tone and often uses the pronoun "we," which implies that you and she are working together cooperatively. She does not attack you or your personality. Mistakes are viewed as just that, mistakes – a temporary unfortunate event – not as a permanent character flaw. Unlike the Bully, the Mentor helps you figure out the steps needed to correct a mistake. When something goes wrong, the Mentor taps into her creative thinking skills and, in a nonjudgmental and noncritical way, becomes a problem-solver.

Your Mentor Doesn't Coddle You

If you ever had an actual Mentor in your life, you know a Mentor will not make excuses for you, nor will she coddle you. The Mentor challenges you to be the best you can be, while still allowing you to be imperfect and human. She encourages you to learn from your mistakes and figure out how to not repeat them. She is firm but in a respectful and caring way.

If you forgot to set your alarm clock and missed an important meeting at work, your Mentor would say, "This is not OK. We need to make sure this doesn't happen again. If we put the alarm clock on our pillow every morning, we will have to set it before we go to sleep. Now, we had better call our boss and apologize right away. Let's also talk with George to get the notes from the meeting."

Stopping the Negative Cycle

So how do you stop the yelling? How do you get the Bully to return to her role as the Mentor? Your other Parts may have tried to shut her up, push her away, get rid of her, or to hate her. This makes the cycle worse; the Bully just digs in her heels and fights for her life.

Actually, you need to do the opposite. Just like the junior-high band needs the teacher's presence in order to get back into harmony and balance, the Bully needs you to be in Self-energy in order to return to her role as the Mentor.

As I said in Chapter 2, your Bully needs and wants three things from your Self: to be heard, to be appreciated and to be taken care of. If the Bully does not feel heard or appreciated, if her needs are not taken care of, she will continue to be extreme.

You need to listen to what the Bully is trying to say – although at first it will be hard to listen to how she is saying it – so she feels heard. Then you need to appreciate what she is trying to do for you – although at first it will be hard to appreciate how she does it. Lastly, you need to take care of her needs – although at first your other Parts may not want to even be near her. The idea of listening to the Bully may make your Parts feel fear, intimidation, hatred, disgust, or anger. Please ask them to step aside so you can get back into Self-energy.

It helps if you remember that underneath all of her nastiness, the Bully is really the Mentor in an extreme role. The Bully has a positive intention and wants something good for you. She wants to help you, but she just doesn't know how.

Think about your own history and background. Did you have any role models who taught you compassionate self-talk, direct communication, respectful language, rational thinking, and creative problem-solving? Maybe not. Instead, the Bully probably learned indirect communication, abusive language, name-calling, humiliation, and all-or-nothing thinking.

Transforming the Bully to a Mentor

Let's look at the steps involved in transforming the Bully into a Mentor. Here's a typical session with Bethany whose Bully is female. Yours may be male, genderless, or even inanimate. Don't worry if your Bully is not cooperative like Bethany's. How to handle Bullies who are downright cruel and nasty will be discussed later in the chapter.

Before we get started, I want to remind you to practice staying in your Self, keeping the teacher in charge of the junior-high band. While reading this, if you feel any emotion except the C qualities of Self – for example anger, resentment, or fear – then another Part has taken over. Breathe deeply, step into Curiosity, Calmness, and Compassion, and, as in the Path exercise, ask the other Part to step aside.

Listening to the Bully

At first I just want Bethany to speak from the Bully so we have a place to start hearing her.

Amy:	"Bethany, let the Bully talk. Tell me what she is saying."
Bethany as Bully, in a loud harsh voice:	"You're absolutely pitiful. Why can't you just be normal? You are just too needy. No one will ever love you."
Amy:	"Where in your body do you experience the Bully?"
Bethany:	"In my head."

The Bully is almost always experienced as thoughts or voices in the head. When very extreme, the thoughts may feel as if they are coming from outside the head, although you are aware that these are your thoughts. (I want to assure you that this is normal, you are not psychotic. Because you are aware of all the various voices, this is very different than what most people refer to as multiple personality disorder.)

Amy: "OK, imagine I can take the Bully out of your head and sit it on the couch across from you. What would she look like if you could see the Bully?"

This is a common therapeutic technique known as the Empty Chair to help you gain distance from the Part and to tap into your capacity for objectivity. Our goal is for you to be in your Wise One Within and, using the qualities of the Self, to listen to the Bully.

Bethany closes her eyes:	"She's really mean looking. She's scowling at me, and shaking her head in disgust."
Amy:	"How old does she feel to you? Is she older, younger, or your age?"
Bethany:	"She feels older than me."
Amy:	"What does she look like?"
Bethany:	"Like a schoolmarm. She's got her hair pulled back in a severe bun. She's wearing a gray suit with a white blouse buttoned tight at her neck. She's sitting very straight."
Amy:	"I'm going to talk to her and I'd like you to tell me what she says. How do you feel about that?"
Bethany:	"I'm scared. I'm afraid of her."
Amy:	"That's OK. Can you ask your scared Part to leave the room? Ask her to go in the waiting room for a while. Give her what she needs to be OK. Tell her it will be all right."

Because it is important that Bethany be in her Self and not allow another Part to take over, I check to find out if other Parts are present or active.

Because Bethany is afraid, an Exile has been triggered. I ask Bethany's scared Exile to "step aside" to allow Bethany to be in her Wise One Within.

Bethany, after a short moment of silence:	"OK. I asked the scared Part to leave, but she wanted to watch. So I imagined she is hiding under your desk."
Amy:	"That's fine. I'm going to talk to the Bully now. How do you feel about that?"
Bethany:	"I'm OK."

I check again to see if there are any more Parts active. In Bethany's case there were none. If there had been more active Parts, the process of asking them to "step aside" would have been repeated.

Finding the Bully's Positive Intention

Next, Bethany and I need to listen to the Bully so we can figure out what her positive intention is for Bethany.

When I use the Empty Chair technique, I turn and speak to the empty chair when I talk to the Bully. When I speak to Bethany I face her. I do this to reinforce the separation between the Bully and Bethany, helping Bethany stay present in her Self. Bethany has the double role of speaking as the Bully but listening as her Wise One Within. Later when Bethany speaks to the Bully, she turns and speaks to the empty chair as well. (Some clients may find it helpful to actually switch chairs.)

Amy to Bully:	"I hear you think Bethany is pitiful. You think she's too needy."
Bethany as her Bully Part, in a loud harsh voice:	"Yes. She's a real loser."
Amy:	"You seem to be working real hard to convince her of this. What are you trying to do for Bethany?"
Bethany:	"I want her to shape up. Stop being such a baby!"
Amy:	"If you were successful and she could shape up and stop being a baby, what would that do for Bethany?"
Bethany:	"Maybe she wouldn't be so pathetic, but I doubt it."
Amy:	"And if she weren't so pathetic, what would that do for Bethany?"
Bethany:	"Maybe she would be more normal. More like normal people."
Amy:	"Yes, I can see that you want her to be more normal. And if she could be more normal, what would that do for Bethany."

Bethany in a regular-toned voice:	"Maybe people would like her more. She might make some friends."
Amy:	"And if people would like her and want to be her friend, what would that do for Bethany?"
Bethany:	"She wouldn't be so lonely."
Amy:	"So if she wasn't lonely, what would she feel instead?"
Bethany in a much softer voice:	"She would feel better."
Amy:	"And if she felt better . . . ?"
Bethany in a warm and caring voice:	"Then she would be happy."
Amy:	"So you are trying to help her feel better so that she can be happy."
Bethany quietly:	"Yes."

Voila! We've found the Bully's positive intention for Bethany. In a twisted sort of logic, her intention is to help Bethany feel better so she will be happy. Remember what the Parts want from us? The Bully wanted us to listen to her and to hear what she was trying to do for Bethany. Because we listened to the Bully, her voice became quieter, calmer and kinder. By listening to her, she was able to move towards the right on the continuum, towards the Mentor role.

Appreciating the Bully's Positive Intention

Now we move towards appreciating what the Bully is trying to do. I encouraged Bethany to be Curious, a quality of the Self, while I talk with the Bully.

Amy to Bully:	"You are working really hard at this. Why are you working so hard?"
Bethany as Bully, her voice is still normal:	"Bethany doesn't listen to me. She tries to shut me up and push me away. No matter what I do, it doesn't work."
Amy:	"If I could help you find a way to get Bethany to listen to you, would you be willing to try it?"
Bethany:	"Well maybe. I'm not sure it would work."
Amy:	"I'll tell you what. If it doesn't work, you can always go back to what you are now doing. You could try it for a while and see what happens, kind of like a science experiment." [Sometimes when it doesn't feel so permanent, it is easier for the Bully to try something new.]

Bethany:	"OK. What do I have to do?"
Amy:	"Let me talk to Bethany a while and I'll get back to you."
Amy to Bethany:	"Bethany, did you hear what the Bully said? She said she wanted you to be happy. Can you appreciate what the Bully is trying to do for you, even though she doesn't know how to do it?"
Bethany:	"I guess. In a way . . . ."
Amy:	"Feel the appreciation deep in your body." Bethany is silent and then nods.
Amy to Bethany:	"Can you tell her that?"
Bethany to Bully:	"Thanks for trying to help me. I appreciate how hard you have been working for me."
Amy:	"She wants you to be happy. Would you like that too?"
Bethany:	"Of course I do."

Negotiating with the Bully

Now we want to establish some cooperation between Bethany and the Bully and work to change how the Bully acts and talks to Bethany.

Amy:	"Bethany, something the Bully is doing now does not work. You are not happy. Would you please tell her how she actually makes you feel?"
Bethany to Bully:	"When you yell at me and call me names, I am miserable. I feel worthless and pathetic. I hate myself."
Amy to Bully:	"Did you hear what Bethany said? What do you think about that?"
Bethany as Bully:	"I know it's not working, but I don't know what else to do. I don't want her to feel bad, but I can't just not say anything."
Amy to Bully:	"Why not?"
Bethany as Bully:	"If I didn't yell at her, all she'd do is screw up! Or else she would just lie around on the couch all day and eat! I can't let her do that!"
Amy to Bully:	"But what you are doing doesn't work either. If I teach you a new way to talk to Bethany so she does listen, then you wouldn't have to yell."
Bethany as Bully:	"OK, how do I do that?"

By this time the Bully has calmed down enough that she can be in her positive role as the Mentor. Bethany and the Mentor feel cooperative and want to work as a team. The Mentor is reassured that Bethany and I are on her side and want to help her achieve her positive intention.

Mentor Whispers and Bethany Listens

We now set up some guidelines for both Bethany and her Mentor. The first relates to the tone of the Mentor's voice. I ask the Mentor to talk calmly and softly to Bethany in order to change the cycle of yelling-ignoring-yelling-ignoring. If the Mentor talks calmly and softly, Bethany promises to listen to her. If Bethany listens, the Mentor will talk calmly and softly. It's a win-win situation.

If the Mentor slips into the Bully role and yells at Bethany again, Bethany is to quietly remind the Bully to talk softly and calmly. If Bethany forgets to listen, the Mentor is to gently remind Bethany to keep up her end of the bargain as well, "You've been a bit distracted lately, let's be more mindful."

Mentor Talks Like You Would to a Friend

The next guideline is to tone down the colorful language. Rather than calling Bethany a foul name, the Mentor agrees to talk to Bethany with respect and kindness. This may feel like learning a new language but, I assure you, you are already fluent.

If a friend had a problem, you would never in a million years look her in the eye and cruelly call her a loser. Even if your friend did something dreadful, you would speak with respect and kindness. You would calmly reassure her that everything would be all right. Compassionately, you would see her situation objectively and creatively break the problem down into manageable steps towards a solution. (Did you catch some C qualities of Self?)

Bethany and the Mentor make a pact: the Mentor will speak to Bethany like she would speak to a friend. In exchange Bethany will listen to what the Mentor has to say to her. In fact, if the Mentor keeps speaking to Bethany this way, Bethany will actually welcome the Mentor's input. What a change.

Developing a Trusting Relationship

Over time you will develop a trusting relationship with your Mentor. At first, she may not trust that you will continue to listen. Just as the first time she speaks softly, you probably will not trust that she has changed. But, as the Mentor sees forward progress (for example, you are not late to work as often, you eat more mindfully and less out of defiance), she can relax; she doesn't have to be on guard as much. As she continues to speak respectfully to you, you learn to trust that she has your best interest at heart and wants good things for you.

Working with More Difficult Bullies

Some Bullies are more deeply entrenched than others. However, with time and patience, they can be transformed into Mentors. Let's look at some more difficult examples.

The Stubbornly Tenacious Bully

Ruth is a very tall, shapely, athletic-looking woman who spent her whole life hating herself and her muscular body. The scapegoat of her family, Ruth was blamed for everything that went wrong, from difficulties with her parents' careers to problems in their marriage. Nothing she did was ever good enough, no achievement high enough, no award special enough, because Ruth's weight negated all of it to her parents, "What are we going to do about Ruth's weight problem."

If that wasn't bad enough, Ruth's older sister Cindy was thin and petite. Cindy hated Ruth and was exceptionally cruel to her. Cindy tried to push Ruth out of a moving vehicle and once locked her in the trunk of the car on a hot summer day. Her parents always sided with Cindy, "Oh Ruth, you're just making a big deal out of nothing." Throughout her life, Ruth felt unloved, unlovable, and unsafe.

The Bully's Positive Intention

It is probably no surprise that Ruth's Bully beat her down unmercifully. When asked what she was trying to do for Ruth, the Bully wanted her to "be small," by that she meant small in size but also small in demeanor. In a series of questions similar to Bethany's example, I asked the Bully what being small would do for Ruth. Ruth as Bully answered, "No one would see her. If she avoided drawing attention to herself, maybe no one would hurt her. If no one hurt her, maybe she would feel safe. If she felt safe, then she would feel better. She would be lovable and happy."

After we uncovered the Bully's positive intention, to protect her from being hurt, Ruth appreciated what the Bully was trying to do for her. Ruth wanted to work cooperatively with the Bully. So, all we had to do was help the Bully find a new way to protect Ruth so she would get a positive outcome for her positive intention. Right?

No way! The Bully was not interested in changing how she spoke to Ruth. I challenged the Bully with the fact that what she was trying to do, while commendable in its intention, just did not work.

Ruth as Bully:	"I'll make it work!"
Amy to Ruth:	"Explain to the Bully how you feel when she berates you and beats you down."
Ruth to Bully:	"I feel horrible when you talk to me like this. I feel worthless."
Amy to Bully:	"Did you hear what Ruth told you? Do you want to find a new way to speak to her so that she doesn't feel this way?"
Ruth as Bully:	"I don't care! I'll make it work."

Amy to Bully:	"I know a new way for you to talk and relate to Ruth so that the two of you can work together."
Ruth as Bully, in a very harsh voice:	"I don't want to change! I'll make it work."

Reasoning with the Stubborn Bully

I try to use an analogy that may help the Bully see the ineffectiveness of its actions.

Amy to Bully:	"You are thirsty. There's a vending machine for soda. You put in a dollar and push the button, but nothing comes out. Would you put more money in the machine? If you were really thirsty, maybe. Let's try four quarters. Nothing comes out. Would you put more money in the machine? Most likely not! Doing the same thing and expecting different results would be like putting in two half-dollars; then ten dimes; then twenty nickels; then one hundred pennies; then three dimes, a quarter, eight nickels, and five pennies and still expecting to get a soda. Eventually we have to admit that we are not going to get soda from this machine and find a different way to get it."
Ruth as Bully, in a loud stern voice:	"I'd kick it!"
Amy:	"You'd kick it?"
Ruth:	"I'd kick the machine and make it give me a soda!"
Amy:	"What if you still got nothing?"
Ruth:	"I'd make it give me a soda."
Amy:	"How long would you kick it?"
Ruth:	"Until I got a soda."
Amy:	"What if nothing came out?"
Ruth:	"I'd keep kicking it!"
Amy:	"But if it's broken, kicking it wouldn't make it give you a soda."
Ruth:	"I'd kick it! I'd make it give me a soda."
Amy:	"You'll be kicking it a long time – maybe forever."
Ruth:	"I wouldn't stop kicking it until I got a soda."
Amy:	"You're working really hard at this."
Ruth:	"I don't care."
Amy:	"It must be exhausting to keep kicking this soda machine."
Ruth:	"I don't care."

Amy:	"What if I told you a different way to get soda? That way you wouldn't have to keep kicking the machine."
Ruth:	"I don't want a different way. I'm going to kick it until I get soda."

Ruth's Bully was very invested in maintaining the status quo among Ruth's Parts. I knew from experience the Bully must be protecting a very fragile and vulnerable Exile for her to be this unyielding.

The Bully's Twisted Logic to Protect Exile

The Bully often criticizes a young Part to protect her from being hurt or rejected. The Bully's warped intention is "If I hurt you first, then no one else can hurt you and you'll be safe." Sometimes the Bully's twisted logic says, "If I beat you down, you won't be confident enough to go out in the world where you might be rejected. Then you'll be safe from harm." In her distorted thinking the Bully thinks that if she can get the Exile to do everything perfectly, nothing bad will ever happen to her again.

I decided to explore this a bit further with Ruth as Bully.

Amy:	"What would it mean if you stopped kicking the machine?"
Ruth as Bully, in a guarded voice:	"It would mean that Ruth was weak and that they won."
Amy:	"What would happen if Ruth were weak?"
Ruth, in a quiet voice:	"They would be right."
Amy:	"About what?"
Ruth:	"That she really is unlovable. I won't stop kicking."
Amy:	"You won't stop protecting Ruth?"
Ruth, in a sad voice:	"I won't stop kicking."
Amy to Ruth:	"Ruth, did you hear what the Bully is trying to do? She's trying to protect you from being hurt."
Ruth in a sad voice:	"Yes, I heard. I never realized that was what she was trying to do."

Because Ruth heard the Bully and appreciated her tenacity to protect her young Parts from feeling unlovable, the relationship between Ruth and her Bully changed. Instead of the Bully kicking Ruth, Ruth imagined the Bully kicking a soda machine. Whenever her Mentor reverted back into the Bully role, Ruth and I would share a smile, "She sure is kicking that soda machine!" Ruth now recognized this was a signal that her Exile was feeling especially fragile and vulnerable. Ruth then knew she needed her Wise One Within to take care of her.

The Puffed-Up Bully

The Bully has a trick to keep herself in control of the other Parts. To get your attention, the Bully can puff up to appear larger, scarier, and more powerful than she actually is.

Joni, whose picture appears in Chapter 4, came to therapy to resolve her issues with binge eating, negative body image, and low self-esteem. One day she described a Bully that she called "The Disgusting Uncle." She saw him as a huge man with rolls of flesh. He smelled bad and had greasy hair and rotting teeth. His nose ran; he drooled as he chewed on a cigar stub. His clothes were covered in food stains and crumbs.

His gravelly voice continually put Joni down for everything she did, from the way she tied her shoes to how much jam she put on her toast. Joni feared him and wanted to just get rid of him. Nothing she did pleased him and he let her know it constantly. When he criticized her, Joni felt dirty, smelly, ugly, stupid, shameful, and no good, down to her core.

I kept reassuring Joni that he was just a Mentor forced into an extreme role and that he did have a positive intention for her. But Joni could not visualize him without being overcome by anxiety. The only way she could tolerate the anxiety stirred up by the Bully was by imagining that I went into another room to talk to him, while she stood outside the door listening.

Finding the Puffed-Up Bully's Positive Intention

The Disgusting Uncle was particularly stubborn in his belief that he had to point out all the bad things Joni did wrong or she'd continue to do them and never be any good. Aha! There was his positive intention. He wanted Joni to be a good person, even though in his black-or-white thinking every little mistake was seen as a major character flaw.

With my encouragement, Joni found the courage to close her eyes and imagine speaking directly to The Disgusting Uncle. She told him that his harassment made her feel worthless, unlovable, and incapable of change. His voice softened as he told Joni he wanted her to grow and move forward in life, to be the best person she could be. He wanted her to be happy and feel good about herself.

All of a sudden, Joni's eyes popped open with a look of astonishment on her face, "He's deflating!" Closing her eyes again, Joni described how The Disgusting Uncle was slowly shrinking like a blow-up costume. Deep inside the folds of the deflated costume was a skinny, frail, and old man who had kind eyes and a sheepish look on his face. She asked him, "Who are you? What's going on?"

He explained, "You wouldn't listen to me when I looked like this. I had to get big, loud, and mean for you to listen. Now that you're listening, I don't need it anymore."

Bully Becomes a Mentor

Joni renamed this Part "Uncle Waldo." With my guidance, Joni and Uncle Waldo had a long discussion about why the previous pattern of communication didn't work. Uncle Waldo wanted Joni to listen to him but, because he had been big, loud, and mean, Joni tuned him out. Because Joni ignored him he screamed even louder. Uncle Waldo wanted Joni to feel better, but ultimately his tirades (as The Disgusting Uncle) had made her feel worse.

Since they both wanted her to feel better, Joni and Uncle Waldo decided to work cooperatively together. They made the same promises that Bethany and her Mentor made: Uncle Waldo was to talk softly and Joni was to listen to his advice. If either forgot and slipped into old habits, the other would gently remind them of the new relationship.

In therapy, Joni realized The Disgusting Uncle started to develop when she was very young. Her mother, an obsessive housecleaner, was exceedingly anxious and rule-bound. Joni was not allowed to sit on her bed or the entire bed would have to be stripped and all the sheets washed. Clean dishes had to be rewashed before being used. Joni often woke in the middle of the night to the sound of her mother vacuuming the same room over and over.

Whenever Joni made a mistake and broke one of the rules, her mother became anxious and started to clean. Joni began to believe, "I'm dirty. If only I was cleaner, neater, good-er, I would make Mommy happy." Joni then scolded herself, which began the polarized relationship between The Disgusting Uncle and her Dirty Exile.

Uncle Waldo, on the other hand, told Joni that she was not dirty. He helped her see that she was normal. It's normal for children to sit on their beds. It's normal to use a clean dish without washing it first. What a relief when she was able to lovingly unburden her Young Exile, "You're not dirty. You're fine just as you are."

Working with Uncle Waldo, Joni's self-esteem and confidence grew. Soon afterwards she had an epiphany: she felt a voice within that told her, "You don't have to hate yourself anymore." She knew deep inside "I am good enough, it wasn't my fault."

Once we changed Joni's relationship with Uncle Waldo, she saw that overeating served as a way to keep her body unattractive. When she stopped believing she was dirty, she felt better about her body as something normal and natural. She started eating mindfully and intuitively and her body responded by losing weight, not a lot of weight, but a little. When she finished therapy, she was in a close and loving relationship with a man who found her beautiful inside and out.

The Protective Bully

If you are a survivor of physical and/or sexual abuse, you may encounter an extremely malicious Bully. Your Bully has the monumental task of keeping the memories, emotions, and body sensations of the abused Exile in check. Your Bully may be heavily invested in protecting you from old feelings that she believes you would not be able to handle. Your Bully may be afraid that if she stepped down from her position of power you would fall apart completely.

Andrea grew up in a chaotic, physically-abusive home. She and her older sister, Fran, frequently witnessed their alcoholic father beat their mother. Often Andrea stepped in to protect her mother. It didn't stop him; her father just beat and screamed at Andrea as well.

Andrea's father also pitted Andrea against her sister by hugging, kissing, and cuddling Fran and saying in Andrea's presence, "Fran is my favorite. Fran is the only one I love." If that was not bad enough, Fran was also cruel to Andrea. She once locked Andrea between the screen and the sliding glass door for hours on a cold winter day.

Because both of her parents traveled for their careers, Andrea and Fran had a live-in nanny, Donna. When her parents were away, Donna allowed Andrea to sleep with her. Andrea felt loved and safe cuddling with Donna at night.

After a while, Donna began to sexually molest Andrea. Andrea was torn by her desire for Donna's attention and affection while, at the same time, she did not like what Donna made her do. Andrea was afraid that if she told Donna to stop, Donna would reject her and withdraw her attention and affection. To solve this conflict, Andrea learned how to "leave her body" during the abuse.

Deep down inside, Andrea believed she was ugly, dirty, shameful, disgusting, worthless, and completely unlovable. She starved herself, binged and purged, and went deeply in debt for several plastic surgeries and liposuctions to look perfect enough on the outside to feel lovable on the inside. But no matter how beautiful she looked, inside she continued to question, "What is wrong with me? Why am I such a loser? No one will ever love me. I am too damaged."

Bully as a Cruel Abuser

In order to stay in complete control of her other Parts, Andrea's Bully took on the speech, mannerisms, and even the appearance of her abusive father. When Andrea's Bully "Raymond" took over, her voice would turn sharp and nasty; a sneer appeared on her face and her body became agitated and stiff.

Raymond was devious in his cruelty to her and switched tactics as soon as Andrea and I figured out the meaning of each one. Raymond ridiculed Andrea completely, cursing and calling her cruel names. After a series of failed relationships with men who neglected and abused her, I realized that Raymond set Andrea up to re-enact her abusive past so he could punish her.

Raymond often urged Andrea to kill herself in order to stop the pain associated with memories from the abuse. When questioned, Raymond said it would be better if Andrea died rather than be powerless and worthless again. I knew it was vitally important to help Raymond find a middle ground between those two options.

Andrea and I needed to change her relationship with Raymond. But whenever we tried to work with Raymond, a wave of fear and dread washed over her and Andrea would lose touch with the Wise One Within. Between sessions, Andrea just fell back into old patterns as soon as Raymond took over.

Raymond's Positive Intention

Because Raymond had a very important job – to protect Andrea's Exile from feeling anxious, helpless, and vulnerable – I treated him with respect. I told Raymond we would not try to get rid of him, that what he did for Andrea was vital for her well-being. But I knew we could not heal the abused Exile unless Raymond was calm and in his Mentor role. If we even approached the abused Exile, Raymond took over with a vengeance.

It took months to uncover Raymond's positive intention for Andrea. Raymond believed that her father was right; that there was something inherently defective about Andrea. One day I asked Raymond, "What if? Just take a moment to imagine what if her father was wrong? What if Andrea really is lovable and her father was the one with the problem and never could see it?"

Andrea's face became sad and her voice softened, "Then why didn't he love me?" Raymond had stepped aside and allowed us to talk to Young Andrea, an Exile who was trying to make sense of her father's behavior.

For months Andrea questioned her Exile's core beliefs, "If I am lovable and worthy, why didn't my father love me?" By using the Wise One's Capacity for Objectivity, she saw that because of his own childhood, her father was mean, sick, sadistic, and just plain wrong. Andrea slowly let go of the self-blame that kept her Exile locked in the shame from her father's abusive behavior. Andrea's Compassionate Wise One forgave her for all the things she did in the past to seek out the attention and affection her young and vulnerable Exile craved.

Compassion for Raymond

Eventually Andrea also began to understand Raymond. She understood that all the cruel and punitive acts were because he was desperate to contain the dire, anxious, frantic, and hopeless feelings of the Exile. Finding Compassion for her Bully's anguish at this monumental dilemma led to a feeling of liberation and forgiveness.

Slowly Andrea was able to stay in touch with her Wise One more and more. She learned to recognize the signals when Raymond was beginning to get nasty; she realized it was almost always in response to when Young Andrea felt vulnerable and needed help.

Recovery Moments

In recovery you will learn to practice your new skills daily. As you do so, you will begin to have "recovery moments," little bits of time when you feel or think differently. You will find yourself breathing into your Wise One several times a day. You will catch a nasty thought and say, "I don't want to talk to myself like that. What would I say to a friend?"

Slowly, as you speak to yourself softly and calmly, like you would to a friend, you will begin to feel like a friend to yourself as well. In Chapter 6 we will go on to explore how to help and heal your Exiles.

Questions to Enhance Your Personal Recovery

Find a quiet time and some privacy to ponder the following questions. You may want to journal what you learn about yourself. I encourage you to share your answers with your therapist.

1   When reading this chapter, did any Parts pop up for you? How were you able to ask them to step aside and allow you to get back into Self-energy?
2   How do you experience your Bully or Bullies?
3   What are some positive intentions you have discovered that your Bully has for you? Is your Bully protecting a younger more vulnerable Part?
4   If you completely got rid of your Bully, what might go haywire in your life?
5   What does your Bully need or want from your Wise One in order to move into its Mentor role? What compromise might you strike with your Bully in order to listen to it?
6   How do you experience your Mentor? Can you think of a time recently when your Mentor was particularly helpful?

6 Healing the Exile

I'm so depressed. Last weekend, I went to my friend's wedding. Even though I had a good time, a sinking feeling came over me. As the evening wore on, I felt more and more alone. I just know I'll never get what my friend has; I'll never be loved like she is. There's something wrong with me deep inside; I'm just not lovable. I've felt it all my life. Even as a child I felt I was a big disappointment to my parents.

Kendra

Can you empathize with how Kendra feels? When I was in the grip of my eating disorder, I sure did. You may experience a trembling of anxiety always just under the surface, a profound sadness and sorrowful grief, or a feeling of being defective down to your core. Maybe you walk into a room of people and feel worthless or filled with shame, "Everyone here hates me. I'm not OK." You might be overwhelmed with self-doubt and distrust all your thoughts, feelings, and reactions. At times you might feel so desperate that you would do anything to not feel alone. Welcome to the tortured world of the Exile.

Qualities of the Kid

While experiencing your Exile can be agony, being in your Kid Part can be great. Your Kid experiences life with all her senses. Excitement, curiosity, awe, and wonder. Playfulness, humor, silliness, the ability to not take things so seriously, it's all from your Kid.

The Kid is usually experienced as emotions and sensations in your body. If your Kid is very young, she may be nonverbal and communicates through gestures, movements, drawings, and facial expressions.

The Kid and Exile Continuum

Just like the Bully and the Mentor, the Kid and the Exile are on a continuum (see Figure 6.1). When the Kid is in balance, she feels content

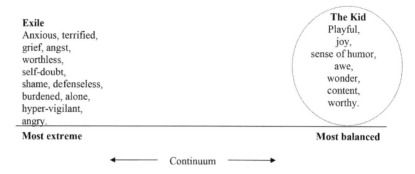

Figure 6.1 Kid to Exile Continuum.

and worthy. The Kid is playful and full of joy. She can make your tasks fun, like the song from Mary Poppins (Sherman and Sherman 1964), "When there is a job that must be done, there is an element of fun. You find the fun and, snap! The job's a game!" If you found yourself humming "Just a Spoonful of Sugar . . ." you are now in touch with your Kid.

The Kid holds your sense of humor and can lighten up tense situations. Your love of learning comes from the Kid who finds life exciting and full of wonder. She can be amused by the smallest things. She likes to be with people, but she is OK being by herself as well.

Qualities of the Exile

On the left of the continuum in Figure 6.1 is the Exile who carries the burdens, memories, emotions, sensations, and experiences of your past. I call her the Exile because other Parts lock her away in a closet to avoid triggering her painful feelings and memories.

Because the Exile is young and doesn't have the tools to handle what life dishes out, she often feels inadequate, helpless, and unable to defend herself. As a result, the Exile is anxious and terrified; everything can feel like a catastrophe. Trying to ward off danger, the Exile is hypervigilant, always on guard. Years of invalidation make the Exile doubt her feelings, thoughts, and reactions.

Just like real children, the Exile thinks she is the cause of all events. It is very frightening to the Exile when she cannot control events, situations, or other people's actions, thoughts, or feelings. Exiles get anxious when bad things happen for no reason other than being in the wrong place at the wrong time.

The Exile blames herself when bad things happen because self-blame feels better than feeling out of control, "If it's my fault, then I can fix what's wrong with me. If it's my fault, I can control everything that happens and make it better."

Just like the Bully, the Exile thinks in terms of black and white, all or nothing, perfection/failure. If even one person does not like you, then the Exile thinks, "I am not likable." If one person criticizes you, the Exile believes, "I am not good enough." Because the Exile thinks like a child, she cannot tell the difference between being liked and being likable, which makes her vulnerable to feeling unlikable or unlovable down to her core if someone disagrees or is angry at her.

Cast out and locked away in her closet, the Exile feels disconnected, isolated, and totally alone in her misery, anxiety and grief.

Core Belief System of the Exile

The Exile holds your core belief system, the messages from your past that you've internalized: the deeply held beliefs about yourself, the basis for your identity, and the definition of who you think you are. Often the Exile truly believes "There's something wrong with me deep inside. I'm really not good enough. I am just not likable or lovable."

You may relate to how Deanna, who you met in Chapter 3, described her Exile's core beliefs:

> Deep in my body, the [Exile] clung to believing I was bad and that all the negative things my father said and did to me were my fault. At one point it just came to me, why I believed these negative things about myself to begin with! As a child I had to believe that my parents were right and good and I was wrong and bad, because the world seemed too dangerous and chaotic to look at it any other way.

Protecting the Memories of the Exile

Carrying your memories makes the Exile feel shameful, disgusting, and worthless. If your memories are traumatic, her feelings and reactions can be agonizing. Your other Parts become invested in locking away the Exile's extreme feelings and painful memories. The Bully harshly criticizes and judges everything the Exile does and says. This reinforces the Exile's core beliefs: "I'm not likable; I'm worthless." Feeling alone, the Exile may try too hard to make other people like her. Appalled, the Bully condemns the Exile even more. The Distracting, Numbing, and Rebellious Troublemakers enter the fight: counting calories, over- or under-eating, angrily rebelling or acting-out.

Understanding the Exile's Anxiety

The Exile's anxiety can be a powerful emotion. When you understand how anxiety works, it is less frightening. With practice you will be able to calm your body and your mind quickly.

Fight or Flight Response

Anxiety is an instinctive survival mechanism that developed tens of thousands of years ago in the most primitive parts of our brains: the brain stem and the limbic system. When Ms Cavewoman was confronted by a saber-toothed tiger, her brain registered a "threat" and activated her fight or flight emergency response. A squirt of adrenaline into her bloodstream made her heart beat faster, her breathing became shallow and rapid, her muscles tensed up, and her senses became heightened, all in preparation to fight the tiger or flee from it.

There were changes in Ms Cavewoman's brain as well. The blood flow to her prefrontal cortex – the area of the brain responsible for analyzing situations, making choices, predicting outcomes, planning, and making decisions – was diverted to the brain stem, which regulates her heartbeat and respiration. Blood flow was also sent to the limbic system, the home of her emotions and memories. Her thoughts raced and her actions were driven by pure emotion and instinct.

Remembering Trauma Ensures Survival

If Ms Cavewoman survived her encounter with the tiger, her brain remembered the experience to guarantee her future survival. She would become hypervigilant, constantly be on the lookout for signs that another tiger was near. If anything reminded her of her past traumatic experience, the memory triggered her brain – Threat! – and a squirt of adrenaline entered her bloodstream. If there was no tiger, the adrenaline burned off naturally from her system in a short while. In the old days, it was better to be safe than sorry.

If you are the survivor of physical, verbal, or sexual abuse, your brain has been trained to be on guard for threats. Just like Ms Cavewoman, if a situation reminds you of a past traumatic experience, the memory triggers your brain to give your body a squirt of adrenaline.

One problem is that the brain has not kept up with the changes in society. We no longer have to fear being eaten by a saber-toothed tiger. An automatic squirt of adrenaline is fine if you are about to be hit by a bus, and it would burn off as you ran across the street. But in most twenty-first-century situations, the squirt of adrenaline is unnecessary, and the effects of it can be frightening.

Additionally, the brain cannot tell the difference between a real threat and one that is imagined. So, when you think, "Oh no! What if I gain weight?" or "Oh my God! My boss won't like me if I complain!" you get the same automatic squirt of adrenaline even though you do not need to fight or run.

Once you notice the beginning symptoms of anxiety – "Oh no! My hands are shaking! What if I have an anxiety attack! What if my coworkers think

I'm crazy?!" – your brain registers another threat, and yes, you guessed it – squirt! – another dose of adrenaline. Your body and mind speeds up even faster and you think, "Oh my God! What's wrong with me? It feels like I'm dying! I must be having a heart attack!" – squirt! – more adrenaline. And on and on it goes.

Anxiety Changes How We Think

The trouble with anxiety is that the feeling of dread and doom feel so real, even though no real threat requiring you to fight or flee is present. If it feels real your Exile believes that it is real, "I feel so awful! Something must be wrong!"

Anxiety thrusts you into the future, "What if (in the future) something bad happens!? What if someone gets mad? What if I get in trouble?" Because the blood flows away from the prefrontal cortex, you cannot think clearly, nor can you remember that you have survived many uncomfortable situations before.

Anxiety makes you lose the ability to discern between the possible and the probable. When you are anxious, it feels as if everything that could possibly go wrong will go wrong. Also, when the Exile is anxious, she believes that she will never feel better again and she will not be able to stand it. This usually triggers the Troublemakers who quickly leap in with behaviors to distract you or numb out the anxiety.

Calming Down Anxious Exiles

When anxious, the Exile needs the Wise One to step in and help her calm her body, emotions, and mind. Your Wise One knows that all feelings – no matter how uncomfortable – will rise, crest, and eventually fade. Feelings are temporary and do not last forever. Your Wise One also knows that you will be able to tolerate the discomfort; you've been through many uncomfortable situations in your past and you have survived every single one.

Breathe into your Self and imagine holding the Exile; speak in a soothing voice and repeat calming mantras to her: "It's going to be OK. I'm here with you. Even though this is uncomfortable right now, this too shall pass. It's OK to ask for help."

If your Exile is too anxious, it may be difficult to get her to step back so you can get into your Wise One. In that case you may need to imagine the Wise One holding you, repeating the calming mantras in her soothing voice.

It is easier to calm down the Exile at the first signs of anxiety. It makes sense to check in with yourself several times a day and, if you are experiencing any tension or worry, breathe into the Wise One and calm the Exile before she becomes more anxious.

If the Exile Were Gone

You might think, "I'm not a child anymore. I should just grow up! Buck up! Why don't I just get over it, move on, let go of the past?" You might feel that you would be better off without your Exile. If you are an abuse survivor, your Exile may feel so much pain and shame that it seems like nothing would go haywire without her.

Well, let's try it. Imagine the Exile was gone forever. What's your first reaction? Relief? Freedom? I'll let you enjoy that for a moment.

But if you get rid of the Exile you get rid of the Kid too. What would happen if you had no Kid inside? Without your Kid, your Mentor would take over and make you be productive and efficient. Each day would be just work, work, work.

Without a Kid, nothing would interest or fascinate you. You wouldn't enjoy anything; you wouldn't find anything humorous or funny. Life would be dull, dry, boring, and too logical and serious.

Without some degree of fear or caution, your Rebellious Troublemakers might act recklessly, thoughtlessly, or irresponsibly. If you never had any doubt, you might become arrogant or overconfident, taking on tasks bigger than you could handle.

Stopping the Negative Cycle

Just like the Bully and the Mentor, the Exile and the Kid want three things from you. The first is to be heard: she wants to tell you her story. Next, you need to uncover what she needs and wants *from* you. (Notice that this is different than listening to the Bully. When you listened to the Bully you uncovered what she wanted *for* you.) Lastly, you will need to take care of her needs.

Just like working with the Bully, when working with the Exile you need to stay in your Self, to keep the teacher in charge of the junior-high band, so that another Part does not take over. By practicing what you've learned in the last two chapters, your Mentor may already be more cooperative and less likely to interfere as your Wise One heals your Exile.

But if, while reading, you feel any emotion except the C qualities of Self such as, for example, anxiety, fear, self-blame, or worthlessness, your Exile is taking over. If anger, disgust, or hatred are present, your Bully is present. Breathe deeply and step into the Wise One. With Calmness, Courage, and Compassion, ask the Part to step aside and give it what it needs in order for you to continue reading.

Transforming the Exile into the Kid

We're going to start with an easy example from a typical session with Bethany again. More difficult examples will be explored later. In the last chapter, when we worked with her Bully, Bethany spoke as the Bully. This time I am going to have Bethany stay as her Self and speak to the Exile as her Wise One.

Bethany came to therapy very upset; she had a huge binge the day before. "I don't know why I did it. Nothing terrible happened. It was just a normal weekend. All of a sudden I just had to go to the store and buy a bunch of food. I felt so alone. After I ate and purged I felt better and calmed down."

Bethany attended a flea market with her parents, an activity they frequently did together. They split up to wander separately and agreed to meet at the entrance at two o'clock. As she walked away, Bethany's father shouted angrily, "Make sure you're here at two o'clock. Don't be late. I don't want to have to wait for you."

While Bethany explored the flea market she couldn't enjoy herself as she felt pressured to keep an eye on the time. To make sure she didn't upset her father, Bethany returned to the entrance 20 minutes early in the cold and rain. "I stood there freezing and wet waiting for them, feeling like I was the one doing something wrong. When they finally showed up at two thirty, a half hour late, they didn't even apologize."

Identifying the Exile

I asked Bethany to imagine herself back in the flea market, to see it and feel it as if it were actually happening. She sat back in her chair, leaned her head back on the cushion and closed her eyes. After a moment she nodded; she was there.

Amy: "Bethany, what are you feeling?"
Bethany: "So anxious, like I want to jump out of my skin."
Amy: "I know it is unpleasant, but stay with that feeling for a moment. Where in your body do you feel it?"
Bethany: "In my chest. I can barely breathe."
Amy: "OK. Feel that in your chest and discern it from any other feeling you get in your chest. [I wait for a moment until Bethany nods.] Take a deep breath and 'step back' from this Part in your chest. See this Part as if it were standing in front of you. Imagine I am placing a magic screen between you and the Part. You can see and hear the Part, but the Part cannot see or hear you."

Until I am sure Bethany is in Self-energy, the "screen" is a way to explore her feelings about the Exile while still protecting the Exile from any hostile or extreme Parts which may have taken over.

Bethany is silent	
for a moment:	"OK."
Amy:	"Let the Part take a form. Who or what do you see when you look at this feeling?"
Bethany:	"It's me when I was a little girl."
Amy:	"How old is the Little Girl?"
Bethany:	"She's about 5 or 6 years old."
Amy:	"What does she look like?"
Bethany:	"Her hair looks matted and greasy. She's wearing play clothes that are quite worn and dirty."

When you first see the Exile, the child may be dirty, messy, and unwashed. The dirt symbolizes the child's shame, "I'm dirty. I'm bad." Despite the messiness, your Wise One knows the child is lovable deep inside.

Amy:	"What is she doing?"
Bethany:	"She's just standing there all alone. She looks really worried. She wants something to eat. She knows it will make her feel better."

Bethany has described an Exile. Next, we need to make sure that Bethany is in her Wise One Within and that another Part is not in control.

Amy:	"I'd like you to just look at the Little Girl and tell me what you feel or think about her. Please tell me your feelings and thoughts, not her feelings or thoughts."
Bethany:	"I think she's really sad. She feels so alone."

Bethany is not telling me her own feelings, she is telling me the Exile's feelings. I want her to separate from and not be overtaken by the Exile's feelings. Rephrasing the question, I ask again.

Amy:	"What do you feel about her that she is sad and alone?"
Bethany:	"She should be stronger. She shouldn't let things bother her so much."

The use of the word "should" warns me that a Bully is judging the Little Girl. If the Bully stays in control, the Exile could be hurt further.

Amy:	"Would you please find the Part who feels the Little Girl should be stronger? Where in your body do you experience that Part?"
Bethany:	"It's in my head."

Because the Part is in her head, this confirms my suspicions that a Bully is active. We need to ask it to step aside so Bethany's Wise One can be present. If the Bully will not step aside we would stop working with the Little Girl and instead work with the Bully, as in the last chapter.

Amy: "Bethany, please thank this Part for her thoughts about the Little Girl."

After a moment Bethany nods.

Amy: "Explain to this Part that while we value her opinion, it is important that your Wise One be the one to talk to the Little Girl. Please ask the Part to step aside."

Bethany: "She went in the waiting room. She wants some time later."

Amy: "That's fine. Tell her that we will talk to her more when the Little Girl feels taken care of."

Because Bethany had previously worked with the Bully, the Bully was able to quickly return to her Mentor role. The Mentor trusted that the Self would eventually include her in the process and listen to what she had to say.

Using C Qualities of the Wise One to Understand the Exile

I check again to see if Bethany is in her Wise One or if another Part is active. If another Part were present, we would repeat the process.

Amy: "Go back inside and look at the Little Girl again. What do you feel or think about her now?"

Bethany: "I feel so sorry for her."

Amy: "Anything else?"

Bethany: "I want to take care of her."

When Bethany feels Compassion or any of the other C qualities of the Self, I know the Wise One is present. Before approaching the Little Girl, I want to strengthen the Wise One to make sure the other Parts don't take over again.

Amy: "Where are you experiencing these feelings?"

Bethany: "Deep inside me."

Amy: "See if you can intensify these feelings. Breathe deeply into the Wise One who feels sorry for the Little Girl. Make the feeling bigger. Allow Compassion to grow inside you."

Bethany breathes deeply. Her face and body relax. Bethany nods.

The Exile Meets the Wise One

Amy: "Bethany, imagine that we take down the screen and the Little Girl is now aware of you. Tell me what happens."

Bethany: "She's a little leery of me. She's not sure if I'm OK."

Amy:	"What do you want to say or do to show the Little Girl that you are on her side?"
Bethany takes a deep breath and is silent for a long moment:	"I don't have to do or say anything. I am just looking at her and feeling love. She is looking into my eyes; she can see my compassion. She looks relieved."

If you have been through very abusive situations, it may take a while for your Exile to truly believe the Wise One is trustworthy. With repetition, patience, and consistency, the Exile will eventually trust that you mean what you say and will not hurt her.

Using the C qualities of Self, in this case Calmness, Compassion, and Curiosity, we explore the events that led up to the binge.

Exploring the Exile's Story

Amy:	"Bethany, let's go back to the flea market where the Little Girl felt anxious. Ask the Little Girl what is wrong."
Bethany:	"She is waiting all alone. She is afraid that they will not come for her and she doesn't know what to do. She's only 5 years old, of course she's terrified."

It's common for the Exile to have an emotional reaction to a situation in the present (in this example, waiting in the cold at the flea market), because the situation reminds the Exile of an emotional reaction to a situation in the past. Carefully, Bethany and I explore this.

Amy:	"Waiting at the flea market made you anxious. Tell me more about this."
Bethany:	"I remember waiting at the flea market and feeling anxious. I was afraid that I did something wrong that made them late. I kept going over it in my mind, but I couldn't let go of the fear."
Amy:	"What would happen if you did something wrong?"
Bethany:	"My dad would get mad and scream at me."
Amy:	"Were you afraid that your dad would scream at you today, or were you afraid that he would scream at you when you were 5?"
Bethany:	"Both, I guess. My dad gets really mad and screams at everything, that's just how he is. But when he screams, I always feel guilty as if it's my fault, no matter what is actually wrong. It wasn't my fault that they were late, but it felt like it was."

Amy:	"Where do you see her now? Is she still at the flea market?"
Bethany closes her eyes:	"Yeah, wait, no . . . I see her waiting for her Dad to pick her up outside of gymnastics class. She's waiting outside and it's cold. She wants to go inside where it is warm but she's afraid if she does, she won't see when the car pulls up and Dad will get really mad and yell at her."
Amy:	"What is she thinking or feeling?"
Bethany:	"She's trying to figure out how to get home if Dad doesn't come for her. She knows it is too far to walk and it's dark out. She knows that she would have to take two buses but she doesn't know which ones."
Amy:	"Does she know why Dad is late?"
Bethany:	"No. Dad was always late. Dad always leaves late and then gets stuck in traffic. Usually by the time Dad picks her up, he is really angry. Dad often yells at her that he was caught in traffic."
Amy:	"How does the Little Girl feel when that happens?"
Bethany:	"That it is her fault. She shouldn't be such a bother." [We have just uncovered one of Bethany's core beliefs: "I am a burden."]
Amy:	"Take a deep breath again. See her with compassion. Do you see it as her fault?"
Bethany is quiet for a moment before answering in a soft voice:	"Well, no. Her parents signed her up for the class. It was their idea, not hers. If it was too difficult to be there on time after the class was over, they could have made other arrangements. One of the other parents could drive her home."
Amy:	"Can you imagine telling this to the Little Girl?" Bethany, with her eyes still closed, is quiet for a while. "She still feels bad. Like she's a bad girl and is going to get in trouble." (Another core belief: "I am bad.")
Amy:	"Do you see her as bad? How do you see her?"
Bethany shakes her head:	"No. She's just a little girl. She's really kind of, I don't know, special. She's smart and resourceful. When she's with her friends she's funny and goofy. [Bethany smiles broadly.] I like her."
Amy:	"Can you show her that you like her?" Bethany smiles. After a moment she nods.
Amy:	"What do you see?"
Bethany hugs a pillow from the couch:	"I've got my arm around her. She's smiling at me. Oh! She looks different. She's not dirty or messy anymore."

Because Exiles are sensory-oriented, use all of your senses when healing your Kid. If you physically hug a large pillow when you imagine hugging the Exile, it will be more fulfilling than just thinking of hugging her.

Uncovering the Exile's Needs

As we unburden the Exile with the compassion of the Self, we help her see herself through the loving, accepting, and validating eyes of the Wise One. The Wise One can separate the Little Girl's worth from what happened to her. The Self repeatedly reassures her that it wasn't the Little Girl's fault; it happened to her, but it was not about her; she was involved in the event, but not the cause of the event.

When we rid the Exile of other's criticisms and opinions, and help her let go of experiences from the past, she often changes appearance. Bethany saw the Little Girl change from unwashed and messy to a child who was clean and wearing nice clothes.

Amy:	"What does the Little Girl need from you right now?"
Bethany is quiet for a minute before she answers:	"She wanted to know that it's not her fault that her father was late. I told her she didn't do anything wrong. I told her that I'm proud of how she tried to figure it out even though she was scared."
Bethany's voice gets softer and she speaks directly to the Little Girl:	"It's OK to be scared. That would be scary for most people. You're not a crybaby because you're scared."
Amy:	"How is she taking this? What's her reaction?"
Bethany:	"She's feeling a little better."
Amy:	"What does the Little Girl want right now?"
Bethany:	"She just wants me to just hold her."
Amy:	"What does she want to hear you say?"
Bethany:	"She wants to know if she is OK."
Amy:	"Can you say that to her?"
Bethany, in a soft voice to the Little Girl:	"Oh honey. You are so wonderful. There's nothing wrong with you."
Amy:	"Does she want to ask you anything?"
Bethany:	"She wants to know why Daddy doesn't love her."
Amy:	"Bethany, breathe into the Wise One again. What do you want to tell her?"
Bethany takes a deep breath, and then says	"Daddy was busy and forgot that you were important too. Daddy had a rough life when

to the Little Girl:	he was a little boy and that made him angry on the inside. It's not your fault. That's just how he is."
Amy:	"What happened? How did she take that?"
Bethany:	"She looks comforted, she likes being with me. She likes my attention."
Amy:	"Just feel that for a moment."
	Bethany smiles.
Amy:	"I'm going to ask you to do something. Don't think about it, just allow it to happen. Switch roles; be the Little Girl. You are being held by this woman who has such warmth and compassion for you."
Bethany breathes deeply. After a moment she begins to cry softly:	"It's such a relief. I don't feel alone anymore!"

By switching roles Bethany experienced the profound relief of connecting to and being taken care of by the Wise One. By experiencing this with her emotions and her senses, the memories and emotions stored in Bethany's limbic system started to resolve and heal. Also, because it felt good to take care of the Little Girl, Bethany willingly looked forward to taking care of her again and again.

Situations That Trigger the Exile's Core Beliefs

After this session Bethany worked hard to change the cycle of bingeing and purging. To remind herself to take care of the Little Girl, Bethany kept a picture of herself as a happy and contented child on her nightstand; it was the first thing she saw in the morning and the last thing she saw at night. She would playfully tap the Little Girl's photo and say, "Hiya cutie!"

Bethany paid attention to situations that triggered the Little Girl's core beliefs of being bad, unimportant, and unlovable. She noticed these arose when others were angry, when she felt left out, and any time she had to wait for someone. Bethany noticed an "ugh" feeling in her chest when her coworkers were talking and laughing together and knew this was a signal that the Little Girl felt anxious and wanted to binge.

Bethany noted that if she was tired or overwhelmed, the Little Girl was extra sensitive and hurt more easily. Bethany learned to plan for stressful events and to soothe the Little Girl beforehand. Breathing deeply and calmly, she compassionately told the Little Girl, "Even though we aren't getting attention tonight, it doesn't mean that we aren't important too. Our turn will come another time."

Bethany noticed that the Little Girl especially had problems when she visited her parents. "Even though I am doing so much better lately with my coworkers or friends, when I visit my parents I can feel myself start to fall apart."

I reminded Bethany that her parents will not recover along with her, and it is up to her to change how she reacts whenever she is with them. Bethany came up with calming phrases to repeat to the Little Girl before each visit. "I remind the Little Girl that I am a grownup, and I do not live with them anymore. I will not let them abuse her. I am in control of the situation and can leave whenever I want."

Calming Mantras

We created a series of calming mantras; reassuring phrases that Bethany could say to the Little Girl whenever Bethany noticed the "ugh" feeling in her chest:

- "You are lovable and important."
- "What you did was fine."
- "I'm an adult now. I can handle this."
- "We're going to be OK."

Breathing into the Wise One and feeling Compassion, she repeated her mantras to the Little Girl in a soothing and loving voice. The Little Girl calmed down, and Bethany's body relaxed.

When the Little Girl felt taken care of, Bethany felt better, her anxiety eased, and the urge to binge passed. Being able to calm the anxious Little Girl by herself made Bethany feel empowered.

The Wisdom of the Little Girl

Over time, Bethany realized that the Little Girl was very wise in her perception of others. Bethany often felt anxious around a coworker, Harry. First she tried repeating her calming mantras to the Little Girl, but she had an important message that she wanted Bethany to hear. Because Harry gossiped, spread rumors, and complained to the supervisor about others, the Little Girl told Bethany to be careful how she spoke and acted around him.

Eventually Bethany found that, as the Little Girl calmed down, she needed Bethany's help less frequently. Each time the Little Girl popped up, Bethany found it easier and easier to soothe her. With consistency and practice, the Little Girl stayed in balance for longer periods. Bethany recaptured the pleasure and youthful energy she enjoyed as a child.

Working with More Difficult Exiles

Working with your Exile may not be as easy as it was with Bethany's. Other Parts may not be willing to step back and allow the Wise One to be in charge. Sometimes you cannot work directly with your Exile and need to keep the Exile in a safe spot for a while.

A Critical Bully Who Will Not Step Aside

James entered therapy because he binged whenever he felt ashamed or anxious. Towards the end of our second session, I asked him to picture the Part who felt anxious. He visualized a young boy and immediately felt disgusted. "That's Jimmy. I hate him. What a wimp! He's repulsive." I knew a critical Bully had taken over.

Male readers may notice that when working with a young Part, other Parts may feel threatened. These Parts may tell you that you're "less of a man." In our culture young boys learn from their families and culture to cut themselves off from emotions, especially vulnerability, helplessness, or fear.

Because James and I had not previously worked to calm the Bully, I did not know if the Bully would step aside. Since we did not have a lot of time before the session was over, I decided to move the Exile to a safe spot.

I asked James to imagine Jimmy as just any child, not himself as a child. This evoked his Capacity for Objectivity, a C quality of the Self.

Amy: "Close your eyes and visualize your apartment. Imagine a door in your apartment that was never there before. When you open the door there's a fun child's room. Everything Jimmy needs is in the room, a bed with soft blankets and pillows. Teddy bears and toys to play with and books to read."

Amy: "Will Jimmy be protected in this room until we are able to get back to him?"

James: "Yes, he'll be safe in here."

The safe room lets the Exile know that you know he's there; that you care enough to want to protect him. The Exile knows he's not alone anymore, and you will come back to help him.

When James saw Jimmy with objectivity – as just any child – he could compassionately comfort and protect him. After a few sessions James's Bully was calm and in his Mentor role, and we were then able to heal Jimmy.

Growing up, James received a lot of cultural messages about what it means to be a man: "Real Men don't cry, feel hurt, or get anxious."

James had a core belief that having feelings is a sign of weakness. He thought that if he ignored his feelings they would go away. Actually, the opposite is true. When James tried to hide his feelings he usually was overcome with shame and anxiety. I knew that if he explored and resolved his feelings, he would feel empowered: a feeling of strength from deep within.

Amy: "Imagine that the Part who is anxious is sitting next to you. Who is it?"

James: "It's Jimmy. He's about 5 or 6 years old."

Amy: "What do you feel or think about him?"

James: "I'm just wondering what's going on with him. He looks so young, so little."

Amy: "Ask Jimmy if he will tell you what is making him so anxious."

James: "He's scared but he doesn't want anyone to know."

Amy: "Why not?"

James: "Well, Dad always yells at him when he gets scared. Dad calls him a 'pathetic loser' and tells him that boys don't cry."

Amy: "What do you feel or think about Jimmy? Is it OK for him to get scared?"

James: "Yeah. He's just a kid. Kids get scared sometimes. He didn't need to be yelled at. He just needed some reassurance that it was going to be all right."

Amy: "Can you give him that reassurance? What do you want to say to him when he is scared?"

James: "Hang in there Little Guy. It's going to be OK. I'm here with you."

As James and I worked together he noticed that his Little Guy stopped feeling alone. When James felt the first signs of anxiety, he would breathe into his Wise One and repeat his calming mantras, "Hang in there Little Guy. It's going to be OK. I'm here with you."

When James accepted that it was normal to feel scared sometimes, his shame diminished. Because he did not have to hide his fear, it was easier for him to seek out other ways to relieve his anxiety; as a result his bingeing decreased dramatically.

Negative Core Beliefs of the Exile

Your Exile carries many negative core beliefs from the past. These negative beliefs can influence how you think, feel, and behave in the present. Ruth – whom you met in the last chapter – was repeatedly physically and emotionally abused as a child. She became hypervigilant, always on the lookout for impending danger. As a result, Ruth's Exile flinched in advance, worrying about the potential risks of every situation to avoid danger and keep herself safe.

In this session you'll notice how Ruth's young Exile uses isolation to protect herself from the possibility of being rejected.

Ruth: "I had a pretty lonely weekend. I stayed home and ate a lot."

Amy: "Did you think of getting together with a friend?"

Ruth: "Well, I didn't want to be a burden to anyone."

Amy: "If you called a friend to meet for coffee that would be a burden to her?"

Ruth: "Yes."

Amy: "Oh? How do you know this?"

Ruth: "I just do. I just feel it."

Your Exile often uses how she feels as proof that her core beliefs are factual and accurate: "If I feel it, it must be true." But, most of the time, what your Exile believes is not true to begin with. These beliefs are based on old erroneous messages, so the feelings based on these beliefs are false as well.

Amy: "Ruth, I know it's not pleasant but feel that feeling of being a burden to others. [I am quiet for a moment to allow Ruth to experience that emotion.] Ask that Part what it would have meant if your friend felt burdened."

Ruth: "I just wouldn't be able to stand it, it would be horrible!"

Amy: "What does that Part think that would have meant about you?"

Ruth: "There's something wrong with me! I'm just not likable!"

Amy: "By staying home alone, what was that Part trying to accomplish?"

Ruth: "I didn't have to feel like I was a burden, like I was too needy."

Amy: "And what was that Part trying to accomplish?"

Ruth: "I guess it wanted to feel safe."

Amy: "So the Part who truly believes you would be a burden to your friend, was just trying to feel safe. She was trying to protect herself from being hurt."

Did you catch the word that triggered Ruth's fear of being a burden? It is a word so foul that you probably avoid it like the plague: Needy. Because it is normal for humans to have needs, what is so wrong with being needy?

In your past you may have received messages that, whatever you needed or wanted, it was too much. "Needy" means feeling like you are too much, too big, too empty, too deficient, just too "Too."

Ruth:	"Deep inside. I always knew I was both too much and not enough."
Amy:	"Too much for who?"
Ruth:	"I guess for my mother."
Amy:	"When you were little, what did you do with this feeling?"
Ruth:	"I tried to not need anything. I tried to not be too much. I tried to not be."
Amy:	"How does it feel to say that?"
Ruth in a very small voice:	"So sad."

Ruth's Exile was stuck in the past and related to her current situation as if she were still a young child living with her critical mother. As in Bethany's example, we went on to make an emotional connection between the Exile and Ruth's Wise One. Ruth let the Exile know that she saw her as a special little girl with many delightful and likable qualities. The Wise One did not see the Exile as a burden, nor as having anything wrong with her. The Wise One did not agree with her mother. The Exile felt relieved to be experienced in such a warm and loving way by Ruth's Wise One.

Once her Exile no longer believed she was a burden – or that she was too needy for others to be around – Ruth slowly took steps to build meaningful and satisfying friendships. If Ruth felt lonely or wanted to isolate, she recognized that her Exile needed reassurance of her worth and lovability.

Exploring Neediness

Because this complete avoidance of "neediness" is so common, let's explore it some more. Imagine you are working outside on a hot summer day (maybe planting that rose bush from Chapter 4) and you become quite thirsty. You ask someone for a drink and they bring you a teaspoon of lemonade. You drink it but are still thirsty. Are you needy? No, you are thirsty. Your need is bigger than the other person's resources. (Quite honestly I would wonder about someone who only offers a teaspoon of lemonade.)

If you were still thirsty, what would you do? Maybe you would drink water from the faucet or go to a store and buy a soda. When you think about physical needs, like thirst, there is no reason for shame – you would just find resources elsewhere.

But when you think about filling your emotional needs – such as a need for comfort, patience, attention, affection, reassurance or love – your reaction is different. When you ask someone who does not have the emotional resources to fill your emotional need, your Exile may be overcome with shame: "I should be stronger. I shouldn't want comfort. I shouldn't have needs. I'm too needy."

There are many reasons why someone may not have the resources to fill your needs, and these reasons have nothing to do with you and your worth as a person. But if, as a child, your emotional needs were repeatedly not met, you may have blamed yourself in order to avoid being hurt and disappointed: "I am too much. I am too needy."

Exile Who Fears She Can't Handle Her Feelings

Another important lesson can be learned from Ruth's example. Her Exile feared she would fall apart, go crazy, or wouldn't be able to tolerate the uncomfortable feelings: "I won't be able to stand it if something goes wrong. I'll feel horrible forever." Ruth's Exile avoided any situation that could possibly make her anxious. Her Exile dwelled on old situations, thinking about them over and over, each time confirming her fears.

Ruth breathed into her Wise One and reassured her Exile that Ruth was an adult who had already survived many uncomfortable situations and, together, they would be able to stand them again.

Exile's Response to Criticism

You may be wondering, "But what if I am not imagining it? What if someone is critical of me or doesn't like me? It does happen, right?"

Yes, you're right. We cannot please all the people all the time. If, whenever you see your mother, she criticizes your hair, partner, job, clothes, and so forth, your Exile's core beliefs are triggered: "What's wrong with me?! I'm just not good enough. Everyone must see how worthless I am." Rather than slipping into old patterns and feeling ugly, hopeless, and worthless, you can respond differently.

When you are with a negative person, remember to breathe into Self-energy. Deep inside, your Wise One knows your Kid is lovable, likable, and delightful.

The Wise One also gently challenges the validity of the Exile's core beliefs. Do these core beliefs reflect your current situation or your inner values? If your Exile believes, "If I gain weight, then I am not lovable" you can breathe into your Wise One and speak to the Exile in a calm and soothing voice, "I believe that it's our inner beauty that counts. You are beautiful to me inside and out!"

Each time you see the Exile through the accepting, validating, and loving eyes of your Self, you slowly change the Exile's core beliefs. As the Kid looks back into the eyes of your Wise One, she feels loved, liked, and valued. She begins to believe she is worthy of love and affection. Slowly the Kid will be less influenced by others' negativity.

Blaming Sexually Abused Exiles

Shelly came to therapy because she binged and purged every night before bed. When she was young she had been sexually abused by her oldest brother. Shelly harbored a lot of shame, guilt, and anger and blamed herself for what happened, "I must have done something to make him do this to me." Whenever she visualized her Exile, she hated her.

In one of our sessions, Shelly had an "Aha!" moment that broke through the anger, hatred, and blame. We were talking about one of her memories with her brother and I asked "How old is your brother in these memories?"

Shelly thought a moment:	"He's in high school."
Amy:	"So what age is that? 14 to 18?"
Shelly looked puzzled for a while before speaking:	"Oh my God! My brother is 11 years older than me. If he was in high school then I would have been between 3 and 7 years old! Oh my God! I was just a baby!" Shelly began to sob.
After a while I asked:	"What are you feeling now that you know this?"
Shelly:	"It couldn't have been me, it wasn't my fault. I was just a child. How could he have done that to me? [Her voice turned angry] Who the hell did he think he was? How dare he do that to me! I was just a little girl!"

By seeing the Exile with objectivity, Shelly was able to feel love and compassion towards the Little Girl, which broke through the blame, guilt, and shame.

Shelly realized her bingeing was because the Little Girl felt unsafe at night. Breathing into the Wise One, she imagined tucking the Little Girl into bed, and telling her "I'm going to sit right here on your bed while you sleep. I won't let anyone hurt you." Shelly was able to make her Little Girl feel safe.

Shelly imagined the Wise One waiting on the bed, watching the door. In her mind's eye, when the teenage brother opened the door, an Angry Part spoke to him in a loud, firm, authoritarian voice, "Get out of here! Leave her alone! What's wrong with you?"

Shelly's Angry Part needed to express her anger in a physical way. In her imagination, the Angry Part repeatedly poked her brother in the chest with her finger as she continued to firmly state, "You don't do that to little kids! She's just a little girl! I'm not going to let you do this to her anymore!" Terrified, he fled the room. (Shelly said the tip of her finger felt sore for the rest of the day.)

Shelly made a bedtime ritual for herself. She imagined herself as the Wise One sitting on the bed protecting the Little Girl, while simultaneously imagining herself as the Little Girl who was being protected by the Wise One. Before dropping off to sleep she told herself, "I am protected. I am safe. I can sleep soundly tonight." Because the Little Girl felt safe and protected, she no longer needed to binge and purge at bedtime.

Extremely Desperate Exiles

Because of Erin's history of sexual abuse, it was very painful for her to even face the Exile who held her most vulnerable feelings. Whenever she tried to listen to "The Girl," as she called her Exile, Erin became extremely anxious. A Bully would jump in and attack The Girl. Erin then needed to back up and work to calm the Bully. Often Erin felt discouraged with how long and difficult the process was, with many ups and downs. One day Erin had a light-bulb moment that helped her see The Girl differently.

All of a sudden, I had a very clear image why it was so hard to approach The Girl. Her need for me was so desperate that she would jump onto me and cling so tightly that she choked me. My survival reflex was to tear her away just so I could breathe!

That was an important realization for me! I saw that The Girl was just a 5-year-old child and not a monster. I thought, 'What would I do if a "real" 5-year-old clung so desperately?' Then, I felt the compassion that I naturally have for all children and didn't react so strongly to The Girl's fears.

It took a very long time for me to tolerate The Girl's feelings. I needed to realize that the danger was from the past and not in the present. Once I understood that, I was able to take care of the Girl.

Exiles Need a Long Time to Heal

Working with your Exile can be scary. Finding safe places and people to support your recovery will ease the process. Exploring your Exile's emotions in your therapist's office can make it feel safer and more contained.

If you were sexually abused, you will need to expect two steps forward and one step back. You may be on the verge of learning something very important, like Erin's light-bulb moment. If you feel impatient or discouraged, or if you worry that therapy will go on forever and you want to give up, please remind yourself: "I can only go as fast as my slowest Part. It will take as long as my Parts need to take."

Your Exile will not be healed by just reading a book. It takes conscious and consistent effort and lots of practice. When the Exile feels safe and protected she will gradually trust that you are on her side, and you will

protect her when other Parts flare up. However, when the Exile feels protected, the other Parts will calm down as well.

When your Kid feels unburdened and safe you will reconnect to an
inner joy and freedom you may not have felt since you were a child.
Michelle describes it well: "Yesterday, I was in [a warehouse grocery
store], and I just felt like doing a cartwheel. So, I tucked in my shirt
and did a cartwheel right in the aisle! It was just a little thing, but I felt
connected to something joyful inside. I felt great!"

In the next chapter we will find the balance with the Troublemakers.

Questions to Enhance Your Personal Recovery

Find a quiet time and some privacy to ponder the following questions.
You may want to journal what you learn about yourself. I encourage you
to share your answers with your therapist.

1   When reading this chapter, did any Parts pop up for you? How were
    you able to ask them to step aside and allow you to get back into
    Self-energy?
2   How do you experience your Exile or Exiles?
3   If you completely got rid of your Exile, what might go haywire in
    your life?
4   What does your Exile need or want your Wise One to do or say in
    order to help him or her calm down and feel taken care of? What
    does your Wise One want to do to take care of your Exile?
5   Can you identify some of the core beliefs that your Exile holds?
6   What are some of the triggers that make your Exile anxious? What
    are some calming mantras that your Exile would like to hear?
7   How do you experience your Kid? Can you think of a time recently
    when your Kid was particularly playful, joyful, or funny?

Reference

Sherman, Richard M. and Sherman, Robert B. (1964) "A Spoonful of Sugar"
from *Mary Poppins*. Burbank, CA: Walt Disney Studios

7 Balancing the Troublemakers

My eating is out of control! We're moving to a new office, and I'm the only one taking any interest in this move. As soon as I get to work in the morning everyone bombards me with questions. I feel so overwhelmed and anxious, like I am going to jump out of my skin. When I can't stand it anymore I just shut down, surf the Internet, and eat and eat and eat! For a while I feel nothing! But then I feel guilty, fat, and ugly. There's got to be another way to handle this. But I don't know how!

Jaime

Sound familiar? Of course it does. You may zone out and feel nothing when eating or exercising, as if you've been washed over by a wave. This is your Numbing Troublemaker, one of the extreme roles of your Advocate.

Or you might notice, "I just can't stop thinking about food, eating, and weight. I just have to calculate every gram of what I eat! It consumes all of my time!" Well, that's your Distracting Troublemaker, another extreme Advocate.

Or if you've ever defiantly eaten or starved when you were mad, then you're aware of the Rebellious Troublemaker, the last of the Advocate's extreme roles.

Characteristics of the Advocate

Who is the Advocate? The Advocate can be the most Self-affirming of all your Parts. The Advocate has spunk and positive energy like a best friend who really believes in you, encourages you, and stands up for you. She helps you assert yourself, to speak up, and protect yourself.

The Advocate encourages you to take care of yourself and to find balance in your life by taking time out, resting, and letting go. The Advocate has a very strong sense of justice, of how people should act and treat each other. She can be outspoken and says what needs to be said.

The Advocate Reacts to Other Parts

When you experience the Advocate she's almost always reacting to your other Parts, to other peoples' Parts, or to difficult situations. Rarely does she instigate problems on her own. When in balance and in her positive role, the Advocate is very subtle – so subtle in fact that you may not even notice her. When all the Parts are in balance, the Advocate sits back, watches, and waits to see if her help is needed.

If the Wise One is in charge and the Kids and Mentors are calm and in balance, the Advocate will be trouble-free. But if you lose your Self, like the junior-high band without the teacher, and if the Bullies and Exiles become extreme in their attitudes, thoughts, feelings, and behaviors, the Troublemakers respond and act out extremely too.

If you've been practicing what you've read in the last three chapters, you may have already noticed some subtle changes. Perhaps it's not as "noisy" in your head; maybe you've felt calmness in your body. Possibly you've had moments of feeling connected to your Self, knowing who you are, or feeling more sure of yourself. You may have felt productive or enjoyed a playful moment. If so, your Advocate may also have already started to become less extreme and more balanced.

The Advocate–Troublemaker Continuum

Just like the Mentor-Bully and the Kid-Exile, the Advocate is on a continuum with the Troublemaker. When extreme, the Troublemaker has three different roles: Rebellious, Distracting, and Numbing (see Figure 7.1).

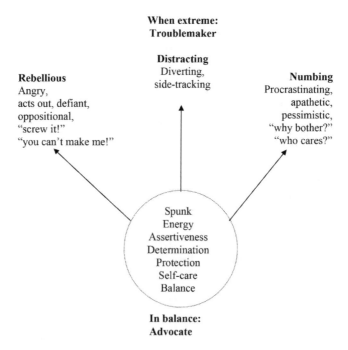

When extreme:
Troublemaker

Distracting
Diverting,
side-tracking

Rebellious
Angry,
acts out, defiant,
oppositional,
"screw it!"
"you can't make me!"

Numbing
Procrastinating,
apathetic,
pessimistic,
"why bother?"
"who cares?"

Spunk
Energy
Assertiveness
Determination
Protection
Self-care
Balance

In balance:
Advocate

Figure 7.1 Advocate to Troublemaker Continuum.

The Numbing Troublemaker

The Numbing Troublemaker tries to get rid of feelings she thinks you cannot handle. When your Exile feels uncomfortable emotions the Numbing Troublemaker steps in: "You don't have to feel this! I can take it all away!" The Numbing Troublemaker makes you eat, starve, exercise, drink, smoke, watch TV, oversleep – anything to feel nothing.

The Numbing Troublemaker often overestimates the intensity of your feelings while, at the same time, underestimates your ability to handle them. She often responds as if you were still a fragile child, not an adult who has survived more than she gives you credit for. If you are in a situation that reawakens old "icky" feelings from your past, the Numbing Troublemaker jumps in: "Oh No! Quick! Get rid of that!"

Listen to Marian describe what it's like for her. "I get a terrible inner churning, like wind howling through my core. I feel anxious, out of control. When I can't calm down, I binge and purge. And there's this calmness. The purge completely takes everything away. But the next day, it all starts up again."

The Distracting Troublemaker

The Distracting Troublemaker diverts your attention from something overwhelming and dangerous to something controllable and benign. Robyn put it very succinctly, "My eating disorder is like a pack of monkeys dancing in front of a movie screen. There's something they don't want me to look at on that screen."

The Distracting Troublemaker has many tricks up her sleeve. Counting calories and fat grams rather than dealing with a difficult relationship. The pressing need to organize photo albums when a big paper is due. Or playing solitaire on the computer rather than writing a book. Oh, those clever little monkeys!

Also, the Distracting Troublemaker convinces you that food, eating, and weight are the problem. If you spend time calculating the calories or fat grams in what you ate, then you don't have to address deeper, perhaps more painful, issues. The Distracting Troublemaker may even convince your therapist to devote a lot of time and energy to talk about food, eating, or weight. "Phew! I got through another session without having to talk about what happened when I was 4 years old!"

The Rebellious Troublemaker

When your Self was sacrificed, you lost your voice, choice, and power. The Rebellious Troublemaker works really hard to help you reclaim those. The Rebellious Troublemaker acts out if anyone or anything tries to control you, especially if they are acting from their own Bully Parts.

If your Bully sets perfectionistic rigid rules on your eating, the Rebellious Troublemaker chooses the very same "bad" foods in defiance – even if you're not hungry.

If the Troublemakers Were Gone

As you've learned in the last two chapters, you don't get rid of your Parts. In order to appreciate what the Troublemakers are trying to do for you, imagine what would happen if they were gone.

Obviously, without the Numbing Troublemaker, the Exile's feelings could be excruciating and even too intense, until you learned healthy ways to self-regulate and self-soothe your emotions.

If the Distracting Troublemaker was missing, your mind would be free to concentrate on other more important issues, "Do I want to change jobs?" "Should I leave my marriage?" "I don't like the way my parents treat me." But, if you didn't have the coping skills and tools to handle these issues, your Exiles may feel overwhelmed and anxious.

What would happen if you got rid of the Rebellious Troublemaker? At first you may think, "If I didn't have a Rebellious Part, then I wouldn't fight with myself so much." But you would soon discover that, without the Rebellious Troublemaker to help keep the balance, your Bully would just take over and intimidate your Exile. Without a Rebellious Troublemaker, other people would walk all over you; you would be the world's doormat.

Without the Numbing Troublemaker the Exiles may not be able to tolerate any of these feelings. Your Bully is triggered, charges in, and takes over. Since there is no Rebellious Troublemaker to make the Bully back off, your emotions quickly get stuck in the same old downward spiral.

Changing the Balance between Your Parts

Over time, the Troublemakers learned to jump in quickly, reacting to any situation that became unpleasant. Numbing, Distracting, and Rebelling became your go-to coping options for anything that life dished out.

In order to help the Troublemakers to change, to find their positive role among your Parts, you need to find the guidance and wisdom of your Self deep inside. Just like the Bully and the Exile, the Troublemakers can't change without the teacher staying in the junior-high band room.

When the Wise One is in charge, and the Mentors and Kids are in balance, the Troublemakers can calm down too. Your Advocates will not need to jump in as quickly, as often, or in such extreme ways. The Wise One knows you can tolerate a little discomfort; and she can help you learn other ways to calm down and soothe yourself. She can teach you healthy ways to stand up for yourself and assert your needs to others.

Balancing the Troublemaker

Let's pick up Bethany's story and look at a typical therapy session when she worked with a Distracting Troublemaker who procrastinated and sidetracked her from her projects.

Bethany:	"I don't know what's wrong with me. I'm juggling so many projects for work, and I just can't get going. I'll play video games, surf the Internet, or text my friends. Anything but what I'm supposed to be doing. I should be working on an important presentation, but all I can think about is how big my butt is getting from sitting so long. I can't stop adding up how many calories I've eaten and how few calories I burn when I'm just sitting. Then I have to get up and walk around. Sometimes I even jog in place by my desk. I can't seem to stop myself."

Separating Out Other Parts

First, I need to help Bethany get into Self-energy and ask any other Parts to step aside. We've already worked with her Parts and have developed short cuts that speed up our work, so it is easier to calm them down.

Amy:	"You sound really frazzled. Would you like to go inside and see what the Parts want to tell us? What they need you to know about this?"
Bethany:	"Yes. I've got to get a grip. I can't keep eating like this."
Amy:	"Close your eyes and go inside. Tell me what you are feeling?"
Bethany:	"I feel very anxious. My chest is very tight. It's hard to breathe."

Calming the Exile

Bethany's anxiety was coming from an Exile. We need to calm the Exile so Bethany can access the C qualities of Self in order to work with the Distracting Troublemaker.

Amy:	"Ask the anxious Part what it needs."
Bethany closes her eyes and smiles softly:	"It's the Little Girl. I imagine telling her I'm going to handle this. That she doesn't have to take care of it. She seems relieved. She's resting on the couch with me now. I gave her a soft blanket."

Finding the Distracting Troublemaker

Once Bethany was able to comfort the Little Girl we were able to return to the Troublemaker.

Amy:	"Good. Now see if you can find the Part who wants to play video games, count calories, or exercise. Where in your body do you experience that Part?"
With eyes still closed, Bethany concentrates. After a bit she says:	"Kind of all over, in my head, in my stomach, my legs."
Amy:	"That's fine. Don't judge it. Take a breath, imagine you can step back from the Distracter, as if it were standing in front of you."
	Bethany nods.
Amy:	"How do you feel about the Distracter?"
Bethany in a loud harsh voice:	"I can't stand her. She's a loser! She is so lazy. She gets in the way and I have to work that much harder to get everything done."

Asking Bully to Step Aside

Since Bethany is not showing any of the C qualities of her Self, I know a critical Bully has been triggered. Again we need to ask this Part to step aside so Bethany can be in her Wise One.

Amy:	"Bethany, it's obvious that a Bully is active right now. Ask her what she needs to step aside so the Wise One can work with the Distracter."
Bethany:	"She doesn't want to leave. She wants to have a say in how I handle this."

The critical Bully and the Distracting Troublemaker are reacting strongly to each other. If I allow the Bully to keep criticizing the Distracting Troublemaker the negative pattern will not change. I use a technique to separate them while still being able to hear what they are trying to do and to uncover their positive intention for Bethany. (Remember, all Parts want to be heard and appreciated for what they are trying to do for you.)

Amy:	"Bethany, imagine standing in a hallway that has many doors. Ask each Part to go in separate rooms. Tell them that you will go back and forth and talk to each of them."
	Bethany closes her eyes and, after a moment, nods.

Listening to the Distracting Troublemaker

Once we had separated but not dismissed the Bully, we could focus on the Distracting Troublemaker.

Amy:	"We heard what the Bully had to say about the Distracter. Look in the doorway to the Distracter's room and ask her to tell you her side"
Bethany answers as the Distracting Troublemaker:	"The Bully is a harsh relentless taskmaster who sets the bar way too high for Bethany. She can never get everything done, and then the Bully says she's lazy and not doing enough. Even when Bethany gets everything done, the Bully just picks everything apart – nothing is good enough, 'The Power Point presentation should have been more creative. The clip art should have been more sophisticated. The font should have been bolder.' Bethany always feels overwhelmed and exhausted. Then she gets depressed and feels hopeless."
Amy to Distracting Troublemaker:	"What Part gets depressed?"
Bethany as Distracting Troublemaker:	"The Little Girl. She feels so worthless. Like she's never good enough."
Amy to Distracting Troublemaker:	"So what are you trying to do for Bethany? For the Little Girl?"
Bethany is quiet for a while:	"I want to give her a break. Everyone needs to rest sometime and the Bully won't let her have fun."
Amy:	"By giving Bethany at break, what would that do for Bethany?"
Bethany:	"Well, the Little Girl would get her mind off it, not feel so bad. At least when I'm around she can have a little fun."
Amy:	"So you're trying to take care of the Little Girl and find a balance for Bethany."

A Rebellious Troublemaker becomes Active

Be aware that more than one type of Troublemaker might be present. In Bethany's case, the Rebel stepped in.

Bethany's voice changes:	"Yeah. If the Bully makes her work non-stop, then I'm going to make sure she does nothing! Hah! In your face! So there!"

A spunky Rebellious Troublemaker who defies the strict rules of the unpleasant Bully has been triggered. We need to separate this Part too.

Amy: "Bethany, we've got another Part here. Did you notice the shift too?"

Bethany nods.

Amy: "Ask this new Rebellious Part to go in her own separate room. Will she do that for you?"

Bethany nods again.

Appreciating the Intention of the Troublemakers

As I said before, underneath the negative behaviors the Advocates are the most Self-affirming of all the Parts. Bethany's Troublemakers need to know she heard what they are trying to do for her.

Amy:	"OK. Did you hear what the Distracter was trying to do for you and the Little Girl? She's trying to protect the Little Girl from feeling worthless. She's trying to give you a break and let your Little Girl have some fun. How do you feel about what she's trying to do?"
Bethany:	"I'm grateful that someone is trying to take care of me. Otherwise I'd burn out!"
Amy:	"Bethany, I'd like you to get in touch with the Wise One Within."
	Bethany takes a deep breath and slowly exhales. Her face softens and she seems relaxed and calm.
Amy:	"Bethany, see the Distracter through the eyes of the Wise One. Can you tell the Distracter that you appreciate what she's trying to do?"
Bethany as the Wise One:	"I don't have to say anything. I just feel grateful in my heart. I can see she knows I'm grateful. It's funny, but I can even appreciate what the Rebel was doing. When push came to shove, she was there for me. She stood up for me."
Amy:	"How does the Rebel react to your appreciation?"
Bethany:	"She feels validated. She feels like I'm listening to her."

Negotiating with the Bully

Bethany and I now need to turn our attention back to the Bully. When the Bully calms down and makes her demands more realistic, then the Distracting Troublemaker and the Rebellious Troublemaker will calm down and be less reactive.

Amy:	"Bethany, see yourself going across the hall to the room with the taskmaster Bully. How do you feel about this?"

Bethany closes her eyes, takes a breath:	"I'm OK. The Bully has been listening. She seems anxious to tell me something."
Amy:	"What does she want you to know?"
Bethany as Bully:	"I know what I'm doing is harsh, but I have to be demanding. In the business world, you're only as good as your last accomplishment. You have to constantly prove yourself. If it weren't for me, Bethany would do nothing! If I didn't harp on her constantly then she would just sit around and play that damn video game! What a waste of time!"
Amy to Bully:	"So you're trying to push Bethany to succeed. If Bethany were a success, what would that do for Bethany?"
Bethany:	"Well, then people would look up to her. They'd respect her and admire her. She would feel important!"
Amy:	"And if others looked up to her and she felt important, what would that do for Bethany?"
Bethany, her voice softening:	"She'd feel good inside. She would feel like she mattered."
Amy:	"And if she felt like she mattered? What would that do for Bethany?"
Tears run down Bethany's face. She answers in a very soft voice:	"I would feel good enough. I would finally feel good enough."
Amy:	"Bethany, what Part is answering now?"
Bethany:	"The Little Girl. She feels so sad."
Amy:	"So the Bully is also trying to protect the Little Girl from feeling not good enough."
Bethany takes a deep breath and slips back into the Wise One:	"Yeah. I really appreciate that all the Parts are trying to take care of her. When they are fighting, she doesn't feel taken care of; she feels worthless and not good enough. But when I take care of her she actually feels cared for and loved. Then the other Parts can just do what they do best."
Amy:	"What does the Wise One want to say to the Bully?"

Bethany as the Wise One to the Bully:	"I appreciate how hard you've been working. I want Bethany to succeed in her career too but not at the expense of her physical and mental health. If you are reasonable in how much you push her, I'll be sure the Distracter and the Rebel won't make her waste so much time. We need to all find a way to work together."

Working Out a Compromise between Parts

Bethany and I then worked out a compromise between the Bully and the Troublemakers. The taskmaster Bully agreed to make Bethany's workload reasonable if the Troublemakers agreed to stop distracting and procrastinating. Since the Troublemakers would have nothing to react to, this was fine with them.

We had to figure out a definition of "reasonable" that all Parts could agree upon. Rather than make a long to-do list in random order, Bethany asked herself, "If I can only get one thing done today, what would that be? And if I can also get a second thing done, what would that be? And what would a third thing be?"

She wrote down the tasks in order and then broke each task into its basic steps. The Taskmaster liked checking things off her list as each was finished.

Bethany reminded the Bully not to call her names and to talk softly. When the Bully stopped criticizing Bethany, her Little Girl was able to enjoy the projects and become inventive and creative again.

Now that Bethany understood what the Troublemakers were trying to do for her, whenever she felt like playing video games or texting friends she knew the Troublemakers were reacting to the Taskmaster Bully. Bethany would take a deep breath, slip into the Wise One and listen to what the Troublemakers and the Taskmaster Bully needed to get back into balance.

Working with a Difficult Troublemaker

Usually, when you experience a Troublemaker, it's in reaction to your other Parts. But sometimes a Troublemaker anticipates potential situations that might cause painful feelings she thinks you can't handle.

Troublemaker Who Anticipates Painful Situations

Emily was in therapy for a while and was doing very well in her recovery. She no longer binged or purged at home or at work. But, whenever she visited her parents, she walked straight to the kitchen and started eating.

Emily:	"I don't know what comes over me. It's almost as if a zombie takes over my mind and body. I feel as if I can't help myself."
Amy:	"Imagine being at your parents' house, feel it as if it were actually happening. What does this Part want you to know?"
Emily:	"I feel like I'm set up to binge each time I come. When we arrive, there's so much food already out, just sitting there. Usually we all just hang out in the kitchen and snack on appetizers."
Amy:	"What are you feeling in the kitchen?"
Emily is quiet for a while before answering:	"I feel dread. I'm not sure what's going to happen. My parents are hard to predict. Is Dad going to drink a lot or not? If he does, what will happen? Is Mom going to be in a bad mood or not? If she is, then who is she going to take it out on? If she's nice, can I trust it? How long will she stay like this before something upsets her?"
Amy:	"Emily, ask this Part what she's trying to do for you?"
Emily:	"She wants to make sure that I don't get hurt. Like taking a pill just in case I might get a headache. Maybe if I don't feel anything, it won't hurt so bad."
Amy:	"Who is this Part trying to protect?"
Emily is quiet before answering:	"It feels as if the eating is to feed a Young Part. It feels very nurturing and inadequate at the same time. The Young Part doesn't really want to eat; she wants to just be protected from Mom and Dad's anger."
Amy:	"Can you appreciate how this Part is trying to take care of the Young Part?"
Emily nods:	"Yeah. I appreciate that she's trying to take care of her."
Amy:	"Emily, take a deep breath and step into the Wise One. What does she want to say?"
Emily:	"We need some more specific ways to deal with Mom so that we're not unprepared for when, not if, she blows up."
Amy:	"How does that Part react to that?"
Emily:	"Yeah! She likes the idea of working together. This feels really good."

Now that the Troublemaker had been heard and the Wise One was in charge, the Troublemaker calmed down. With the help of the Wise

One, Emily's Troublemaker could step into her positive role and, as the Advocate, work on self-care, problem solving, and balance.

Emily and I worked on some practical strategies for when she visited her parents. First, Emily planned out her visits in advance. She arranged to arrive when her mother was "fresh," before her siblings and their families arrived. Second, she made sure she was not hungry, which was a sure set-up to binge.

Third, as Emily got out of the car, she told her Young Part that she loved her no matter what and imagined letting her play outside. Fourth, as she entered the house, she breathed into the Wise One and reminded her Parts that she was an adult and had many resources available to her. Last, when she noticed her mother getting "that look," Emily would make an excuse to leave the room: go to the bathroom, go outside, take a walk around the block, or play with her nieces and nephews. She reminded herself that she could leave any time she wanted, even if her mother didn't like it; she was not trapped at her mother's house.

Because Emily was aware of the underlying reasons for bingeing, and had found strategies to deal with the feelings that arose during her visits, the "zombie eating" diminished almost entirely.

Rebellious Troublemaker Who Takes Care of the Powerless Exile

Let's look at another example. Jasmine was in therapy for bulimia. She and her father worked for the same company. When she was a child, her father ignored and neglected Jasmine. He also physically and verbally abused her.

Jasmine:	"My father just retired and the company was planning a big party to give him an award. Everyone has been saying great things about him. I just smile and nod, but inside I want to scream what a jerk he really is! If they really knew how badly he treated me when I was little, they wouldn't think he was so great. On the evening of the party, I bought a lot of food, some beer, and a pack of cigarettes, even though I haven't smoked in five years. I didn't go to the party. No, I stayed home, got drunk, smoked, and ate. Hah! That's what I think of your big award, Dad!"
Amy:	"Jasmine, take a deep breath and go inside. Find the Part who bought the food and stayed home to eat."
Jasmine stares off into space and is quiet for a while:	"It's Jazz, that's what my friends called me in High School. She's really pissed."

Amy:	"Look at Jazz for a while. What do you think or feel about her?"
Jasmine:	"I like her. She's pretty gutsy."
Amy:	"Ask Jazz what she needs you to know."
Jasmine stares off for a while before answering:	"She's really mad at Dad. And she's really mad that no one else can see what he's really like! It makes her angry that so many people are fooled by how fake he is."
Amy:	"Ask Jazz to show you something about that."
Jasmine:	"She's showing me times when I was younger that Dad was so mean to me and no one did anything about it. So, I would sneak into his room and steal money, go to the store, buy a lot of food, and eat."
Amy:	"Sounds like what happened last weekend. Ask Jazz what she was trying to do for you?"
Jasmine closes her eyes:	"She wants me to not feel so helpless. It was a way to feel like I was getting back at him."
Amy:	"What would have happened if you had stood up to Dad when you were young?"
Jasmine:	"Oh no! That would have been much worse! He would have beaten me for sure!"
Amy:	"Sounds like you were stuck between a rock and a hard place."
Jasmine:	"Yeah. There's a Young Part feels completely powerless. She was really scared of him."
Amy:	"Ask Jazz to tell you what she was trying to do for the Young Part?"
Jasmine as Jazz, her voice sounds a bit sassy:	"Well someone had to do something. He shouldn't have been allowed to get away with how he treated her. When I took money from his room, it made me feel like I had some power over him."
Amy to Jazz:	"And when you feel like you have power over him, what does that do for Jasmine?"
Jasmine as Jazz:	"She feels important, like she can punish Dad. She has some power and control over him."
Amy:	"But Jasmine is important now. She's a grown adult."

Jasmine looks puzzled before answering, no longer in Jazz's voice:	"Wow, I realize something! Jazz and the scared Young Part don't know that. They're still stuck in the past. When my coworkers praised Dad, I felt like when I was very young. The scared Young Part felt all alone again. Like no one even knows or cares she's hurting."
Amy:	"Jasmine, does your reaction to your father's party make sense to you now?"
Jasmine:	"I guess I was trying to punish Dad again. But I took it out on me and the sad thing is that he didn't even know it."
Amy:	"Take a deep breath and go deep inside to the place of peace within. Listen to the voice of the Wise One. What do you hear?"
Jasmine:	"She feels sorry for the scared Young Part. She wants to hold her and tell her that Dad was wrong to be mean to her."
Amy:	"Feel that with your body as if it were actually happening."
Jasmine puts a cushion in her lap and hugs it. She closes her eyes and is silent for a while:	"The scared Young Part wants to know why Dad was mean to her? Is she bad?"
Amy:	"What do you want to tell her?"
Jasmine to the Young Part in a soft soothing voice:	"No. He's just a broken person who doesn't know how to love. You're just a little girl. You don't deserve to be hurt like this."
Amy:	"How is she reacting?"
Jasmine:	"She likes to hear it. She feels like someone finally cares."
Amy:	"Feel that for a moment. Allow her to feel your care."
	Jasmine silently smiles.
Amy:	"Keep holding her, but let's also turn back to Jazz. When people talk highly of your Dad, what does Jazz need in order to not take it out on you or your body?"
Jasmine:	"If the Young Part is taken care of and protected, Jazz is OK. She wants to do something though, something that has true meaning."
Amy:	"Ask her what that means for you."
Jasmine:	"She wants to do something that will make a difference in a child's life. She also wants to send a message to Dad that what he did is not OK."

When Jasmine's Young Part was taken care of, her Rebellious Troublemaker calmed down and was able to slip back into her positive role as the Advocate. Her Advocate wanted Jasmine to reclaim her voice and speak out against child abuse. She joined Big Brothers/Big Sisters (www.bbbs.org) and became involved in the life of a young girl from an abusive family. Jasmine not only healed her abused Young Part, she made a difference in another child's life as well.

A Troublemaker Who Needs to Be Heard

Rebecca came to therapy to work on her overeating. She realized that sometimes she over-ate because she was anxious, but other times she over-ate to push down a deep sense of not getting what she wanted in life.

Rebecca had a smart-mouthed in-your-face "party girl" Rebellious Troublemaker whom she referred to as Roxy. As I said before, the Troublemakers and Advocates can be the most self-affirming of all the Parts and often have important messages that you need to hear. If you don't listen, the Troublemakers can get quite insistent; their behavior may escalate until you have to hear them.

In this example, listen to how Rebecca tries to speak from her Rebellious Troublemaker, but every other sentence is a different Part who tries to censor her.

Rebecca, talking very fast, gesturing wildly with her hands:	"I've been all riled up. Every day! Roxy keeps going off on people. I know I'm the better person so I should take it. But I've reached a peak! I'm not going to take other people's sh*t all the time. But I know I should be more subdued. With my parents, usually I'm quiet, but Roxy won't stop talking. My fiancé and my sister interrupt me all the time, and Roxy just gets so mad at them. My boss is a jerk. I shouldn't say no to him because he's my boss, but Roxy just told him off. I have to take it from the customers; I'm professional and all that. But in the backroom, Roxy just lets it all out. My coworkers like it and egg me on."
Amy:	"Whoa! Rebecca, slow down. Take a breath."
Rebecca:	"Yeah, I know I should just shut up."
Amy:	"No, far from it. I think Roxy has something she wants you to know. As you know, all our Parts want to be heard. The last thing you need to do is shut Roxy up!"
Rebecca:	"But Roxy picked a fight with a woman on the bus. The woman was talking real loud on her cell phone while she was cracking her gum. It was

disgusting. Roxy got in her face and called her names. The woman was a tough b**ch and started screaming at me. I can't be doing this, it's not safe. If she had a gun she could have shot me."

Amy: "I hear you. Rebecca. You know this isn't really about the woman cracking her gum. That was just the last straw. What were the other straws? What does Roxy really want to tell you? What does Roxy need you to know?"

Rebecca as Roxy: "I'm not being heard! Everyone is telling me to shut up. To be subdued. I'm not getting my share! Why should I move on the bus?! When is it going to be my turn? When do I get heard!?"

Amy to Roxy: "Roxy, what do you want for Rebecca?"

Rebecca: "I want the whole world for Rebecca. I want her to have a better life without worrying about money. I want her to have a more fulfilling relationship. A rewarding career. I want her to leave waitressing to move on to the next thing. She wants to open her own business, be her own boss, be respected by others. But she's still doing grunt work."

Amy: "Is there something else you want to tell Rebecca?"

Rebecca: "I'm mad that she's not listening to me! She won't let me speak!"

Amy: "Tell her more about that."

Rebecca: "She used to let me write rap music. I'd write lyrics about what made us mad. About how to change the world. She hasn't let me do that in a long time. Now, it's all bottled up inside until I can't stand it anymore."

Amy: "What do you want from Rebecca?"

Rebecca: "I want her to listen to me more often rather than pushing me down. When she's so professional all the time, she can't say what she's really thinking. She's afraid to speak up to her boss because right now she needs the money. She knows she's really above this job. I want her to take more steps to make her new business a reality."

Amy: "Rebecca, did you hear what Roxy was saying?"

Rebecca: "Yeah. I hear her."

Amy: "Rebecca, Roxy knows that your job isn't giving you what you want in life. Can you appreciate what Roxy is doing for you?"

Rebecca, with tears in her eyes, nods: "She's trying to save me. She's trying to give me Rebecca back."

I encouraged Rebecca to take a deep breath, go inward and find the Wise One Within. Using the C qualities of Compassion, Curiosity, and Creativity, Rebecca and Roxy worked together to find a balance. Rebecca promised to give Roxy more opportunities to express herself. In exchange, Roxy promised not to "go off" on others inappropriately, as long as Rebecca listened to her. We spent several sessions practicing ways for Rebecca to express herself to her family members and fiancé.

When Rebecca began researching opening her own business, an Exile became very anxious. Rebecca's Wise One Within reassured the Exile that she would take it slow and not make any rash decisions.

Rebecca and Roxy worked together cooperatively, and Rebecca appreciated Roxy's presence in her life. "She makes me feel alive! She's spunky and a lot of fun!"

Switching Symptoms and Behaviors

Troublemakers sometimes cause problems by switching behaviors and symptoms. If you stop eating compulsively, you find that you are drinking more. When you control your drinking, suddenly you have to smoke pot. When you give up smoking pot, your eating wreaks havoc again. You may think, "I just have an addictive personality."

When you have a firm sense of Self and all of your Parts feel heard, appreciated, and taken care of, then the Troublemakers won't need any of these behaviors. But if your Bullies and Exiles are out-of-control, the Troublemakers will keep reacting.

You met Molly in Chapter 4. She restricted during the day and binged at night in order to deal with an abusive relationship with her boyfriend Sean. Molly drank heavily and smoked marijuana several nights a week. She also chain-smoked cigarettes and exercised compulsively almost every day. Whenever she tried to control one symptom, another took over.

Amy:	"Imagine the Part who binges, drinks or smokes."
Molly closed her eyes:	"It looks like a little green Gremlin. He's really gruesome."
Amy:	"What do you think or feel about the Gremlin?"
Molly:	"I don't like him. I'm scared of him. I want him to just go away."
Amy:	"Well, we need to find out what he's trying to do for you."
Molly seemed very afraid as she answered:	"I don't want to talk to him."

Just like Joni's puffed-up Bully in Chapter 5, in order to keep Molly under his control, her Troublemaker had taken the form of a scary Gremlin.

I knew that, underneath the gruesome exterior, the Troublemaker was trying to do something positive for Molly.

Amy:	"Molly, take a few deep breaths. See if you can be curious about what the Gremlin is going to tell us." [Remember, Curiosity is a C quality of the Self.]
Amy to Gremlin:	"You're working really hard. What are you trying to do for Molly?"
Molly as Gremlin:	"Molly's such a wimp. Someone has to take care of her."
Amy:	"So you're trying to take care of her. Tell me more about that."
Molly:	"I don't think she would be able to take it if she knew all about it."
Amy:	"All about what? What don't you want her to know?"
Molly:	"Well, if she took a good look at her life, she'd get really depressed. Sean is abusive, her job sucks, her parents treat her like cr*p, and her best friend just uses her."
Amy:	"So you keep her from looking at things that would cause her to get depressed?"
Molly:	"Yeah."
Amy:	"What do you think would happen if she got depressed?"
Molly:	"Well, either she'd fall apart or . . . she'd get really angry! She'd be so angry she'd destroy everyone!"

Molly never learned to express anger in healthy ways. When she tried to express her emotions to Sean, her parents, or her friends, they attacked her back. So Molly feels angry, stuck, and frustrated. The Troublemaker tries to deal with Molly's anger and frustration by turning to food, alcohol, pot, cigarettes, and exercise.

Eating, drinking, smoking, or getting high triggers Molly's Bully: "You're a pig! You shouldn't have eaten that! What's wrong with you? Tomorrow you only get salad."

Molly needs to recognize when she is angry and find other ways to deal with her emotions, then the Gremlin will not have to resort to destructive behaviors.

Amy to Gremlin:	"Wow, that's a big job. No wonder you're working so hard."
Amy to Molly:	"Molly, did you hear what the Gremlin is trying to do for you? How do you feel about the Gremlin now?"

Molly:	"He's a lot less gruesome. He's not so scary."
Amy:	"Can you appreciate what he's trying to do for you?"
Molly:	"Yeah."
Amy:	"How would you tell him or show him your appreciation?"
Molly closes her eyes for a moment before answering:	"He knows."

As described in Chapter 4, Molly slowly and gradually established her sense of Self; she was able to assert herself and make real changes in her life. Then she was able to stop bingeing without resorting to drinking or smoking.

Self-Injury

If you were sexually abused, your Troublemakers will be much more invested in protecting your Exile from the feelings, memories, emotions, and body sensations of the abuse. Your Troublemakers are afraid you will not be able to handle these feelings. They worry that you will fall apart and not be able to put the pieces back together again. The Troublemakers may resort to self-injury in a frantic attempt to keep you away from the closet where your Exile has been banished. "OMG! She's going near the closet! Quick, make her stop!"

Please be patient with the pace at which your Parts need to work. You can only go as fast as your slowest Part. If you charge in to get at the root of the sexual abuse too fast, the Troublemakers may escalate their behaviors, resorting to self-injury or other abuse to your body. I encourage you to seek out a therapist who has experience working with sexual abuse survivors.

Erin, whom you have met in several chapters, worked very hard in therapy for many years to overcome both her eating disorder and her self-injury behaviors. Erin graciously agreed to write about her journey to full recovery. Her eloquent explanation (and my comments) follows:

In order to stop the self-injury, the first step was to allow myself to look at all those weak, vulnerable, very young Parts who were so very hard for me to face. I believe it's because, for so long, I blamed them for all of the abuse. Instead of facing the hurt and pain of my childhood, it was easier to blame the Little Girls every time one of them surfaced.

Even though Erin says "the first step," this actually happened after years of therapy. She had to build up enough Self-energy to be able to work with the desperate Little Girls. By stepping back from these Little Girls and staying in her Self, the Wise One was able to compassionately heal the Little Girls' wounds.

> Because I couldn't face the Little Girls' vulnerability, another Part developed into an [abusive Troublemaker]. Every time I felt vulnerable, the [Troublemaker] would surface and squash the vulnerable Little Girls down through self-injury.
>
> I needed to understand, both intellectually and, more importantly, empathically, that the sole purpose of the [Troublemaker] was to protect me from the painful emotions these Little Girls carried. When I finally was able to listen to the Little Girls, which was my only way out of the self-injury, I had to work hard to keep the [Troublemaker] quiet enough to hear them. I had to assure the [Troublemaker] that, with the help of the Wise One, I would be strong and not get destroyed by drowning in the emotions.

Erin needed to have the strength and courage from her Self to not get sucked into the extreme emotions and sensations stirred up by working with the Little Girls. It was only then that the Troublemakers could trust Erin enough to allow this work to proceed.

> My recovery took a very long time. I was fortunate to be able to find and work with some very good people. I think one thing I learned in therapy occurred without my even knowing. By observing the empathy of those I was leaning on, I eventually was able to have empathy for the Little Girls who needed help.

Therapists who work with sexual abuse survivors must be able to be in their Wise One and not allow their own Parts to become activated and take over in the session. The compassionate healing power of the therapist's Wise One is a very important component in the healing process.

> Another very important thing I learned is to stick with it when I didn't see growth, didn't understand growth, and didn't even know if I wanted growth! I've come to believe that the seemingly non-productive boring phases were times of great growth. Growth doesn't come out of a vacuum but is a result of all the tiny baby steps of progress.
>
> How I stopped the self-injury is a hard question. I wish I could say that I just woke up one day and didn't need to do those things. But, the truth is, as I got closer and closer to trusting all the things I'd observed and learned, eventually I had to take proactive steps – and, as much as I didn't want to, I had to do the work! I had to put all the thoughts and feelings to the test and resist the almost

knee-jerk reactions of self-injuring. I had to talk myself through making different choices. At the time it seemed like making different choices was not real. But the more I did it, the easier it was to realize different choices were not only possible, but were the way out of the trap I had been living in for so long.

As Erin said, you're not going to just wake up one day and suddenly become different. I know you want that; I wanted it during my recovery too. Yes, it takes work. It takes proactive steps. It takes resisting knee-jerk reactions. But slowly, slowly, you'll notice it all falling into place. Once the teacher stays in the junior-high band room, she and the musicians gradually get into harmony together – and it will be beautiful.

In the next chapter let's look at what's really important.

Questions to Enhance Your Personal Recovery

Find a quiet time and some privacy to ponder the following questions. You may want to journal what you learn about yourself. I encourage you to share your answers with your therapist.

1   When reading this chapter, did any Parts pop up for you? How were you able to ask them to step aside and allow you to get back into Self-energy?
2   How do you experience your Troublemakers?
3   If you completely got rid of your Troublemakers, what might go haywire in your life?
4   What do your Troublemakers need or want your Wise One Within to do or say in order to help them move into their Advocate roles? What does your Wise One want to do or say to your Troublemakers?
5   What are your Troublemakers trying to do for you? What are their positive intentions?
6   When your Advocate is in balance, what is that like for you? Think of times you've found balance, spoken up about a situation, did a self-care activity, and so forth.

8 What Do You Value?

Stop reading; get a pen and several sheets of paper. Sit comfortably, close your eyes and take a deep breath.

Get out of your head and, for a moment, suspend all thinking. Breathe deeply; turn off all judgments, criticisms, worries, cares, and fears. Go inward to the quiet place of peace inside you, to the calm voice of wisdom that knows what is right and best for you. From this place of peace, wisdom, and knowing, let the answers to the following three questions just bubble up from within. Write down the answers that pop up immediately.

1   Imagine you are 101 years old and this is the last day of your life. You are lying in your deathbed surrounded by all of your loved ones, friends, and family. The room is packed. Among those gathered are some whom you haven't met and even some who haven't been born yet. What do you want and need to do between now, the day you are reading this book, and the day that you are 101, in order to lie back on your death-bed and say with satisfaction, "Ah! That was a good life! Thanks!"

2   It is the day after your death and your memorial service, wake, or funeral is taking place. Imagine your loved ones, friends, and family members as each steps up to give your eulogy. What do you want them to say about you and your life? How do you want them to remember you?

3   It is today – the day you are reading this book. You just found out that you have only six months to live. (Don't worry. You will feel fine and will be active until you die quickly and painlessly in your sleep.) Knowing this, how would you spend the next six months?

Clarifying Your Values and Goals

The exercise you hopefully just completed helps you clarify what is really important to you; it illuminates your values and goals.

I ask my clients these questions towards the beginning of therapy. In the session we discuss the answers that pop up immediately. Then I encourage them to ponder the questions until our next session to get to the deeper answers. I encourage you to spend some time pondering the questions and then write out your answers if you haven't already done so.

You may have very specific goals, like Leah: "I want to speak French fluently, live in Paris, and work for the American embassy as an interpreter." Or your goals may be vague. You may want to have a satisfying career and fulfilling friendships. You may want to travel, have adventures, and enjoy doing fun things. You may know you want to be in a committed relationship or have children. You may want to make the world a better place, leaving your mark and helping others.

You probably want your loved ones to remember you as being generous, loving, kind, strong, resilient, fun, humorous, and a warm, trustworthy, and caring friend. For the last six months of your life you undoubtedly would do the things you always wanted to do: travel, take risks, have fun. You most certainly want to take the time to tell your friends and family you love them.

What's Really Important to You?

In over 30 years of practice, not once has a client said "My only life goal is to be the skinniest person in the world. I want my friends to remember I wore a size 0. I'd spend the last six months of my life exercising and starving myself. On my tombstone I want it to say, 'She Lost xx Pounds.'"

When I introduced this exercise to Julie, who was just beginning her recovery from anorexia, she made a list of what she wanted from her life:

1 Being a kind, fun, caring person who enriches the lives of others with my presence.
2 Continued education – deepen my intelligence.
3 Being at peace with myself and the world.
4 Having a long, healthy life.
5 Being a good friend, sister and daughter.
6 Creating, in my lifetime, something unique and lasting that can be enjoyed by others.

As Julie read her list to me, she began to cry: "Not a single goal has anything to do with my physical appearance. I'm so frustrated that I spend at least 95 percent of my day and my brainpower thinking about something so insignificant."

Another client, Marian, also considered these questions. "I'd like to be at peace, to be able to enjoy myself when I am totally alone; to just 'be.' On the other side of the coin though, I'd like to be able to bond with people more fully. I want people to remember my sense of humor, how I made them laugh, how they made me laugh."

Then Marian remembered a conversation with some friends at a party. "We were all talking about what was the most important thing in our lives. Most of us said our family, our friends; some felt strongly about their careers. But one woman said, 'My clothes. My jewelry.' I felt really sad for her. When she dies, her jewels aren't going to come to her grave and cry. Her clothes aren't going to miss her when she's gone."

When Meaning and Purpose Get Lost

When you are in the midst of your eating disorder, food, eating, weight, and appearance are very important to you. As noted in Chapter 1, when you sacrificed your Self, you felt as if there was nothing inside of you. So your outside – your size, shape, and appearance – became crucial.

But, more importantly, when you sacrificed your Self, you lost the meaning, direction, and purpose of your life. You lost the connection with what you really value deep inside. You lost your voice, your choice, your personal power.

As you recover your Self, you will learn to live each day according to your own beliefs and values, with a direction and purpose to achieve what is important to you deep inside.

How Do You Live Your Life?

In January 1999 an article in The Awakening Center newsletter stated: "In 1990, Americans spent $33 billion per year supporting the dieting and weight loss industry." Most people cannot comprehend the enormity of that amount: $33,000,000,000. That's $33,000 times a million. (As I write this book in the year 2016, Americans spend more than $50 billion on dieting and an additional $10 billion on cosmetic surgery and liposuction.) In the newsletter article we asked our readers: "Think about the good you could actually do for the world with this money. If you had $33 billion, what would you do with the money?"

We received many interesting replies. One reader sent us a lengthy but specific plan. She wanted to give $1 million each to a list of charities. She wanted to pay off her parents' mortgage and buy her grandmother a house. She wanted to get her graduate degree. We estimated how much all of that would cost and we wrote back to ask, "What would you do with the other $32 billion dollars?" Even with the lengthy list of charities, the reader couldn't fathom how much money $33 billion actually is.

What Are the Deeper Issues?

On the night of September 11, 2001 our eating disorder drop-in support group met as usual. Driving to the group felt surreal in light of the terrorist attacks on the World Trade Center and the Pentagon earlier that day, I wasn't sure if anyone would show up. I was surprised to see there were more members than usual.

That meeting was unlike any other support group meeting I had ever led. The members didn't talk about the usual concerns about food, eating, or weight. We talked about fear and safety, vulnerability and risk, connection and loneliness, life and death. The members were so open and honest with one another.

One member commented, "Sometimes I get so hung up on if I ate a cookie. But, nothing in life is guaranteed at all. We really only have today. There's so much out there that we don't know. Right now, the size of my thighs is really so unimportant."

How Do You Want to Use Your Resources?

If you think about it, you have only four resources available to you: time, energy, money, and intelligence. When you are aware of your values and life goals, you can then decide how you want to spend your limited resources. Because you only have so many hours in a day, so much money in your bank account, so much energy to spend, what do you want to do with these?

As Julie progressed in her recovery, she found that getting in touch with her Wise One helped her make mindful decisions each day.

To me, using my resources is like saving money for a vacation next summer. Yes, I could spend a few dollars now on something that's not really very important to me, or I could stop and remember my long-range plans.

When I think of skipping meals, I remind myself what's really important to me in the long run. Yes, I could spend my time, energy, and money on losing weight, or I can breathe in and listen to my Wise One. She tells me that acting on my urge to restrict really is just continuing to hate the Little Girl inside me. I need to love that Little Girl. I need to think of how I want to live my life in the long run, not just my size, weight and appearance today.

Whenever I think, 'Oh my God! I'm going to gain weight' I breathe in and listen to my Wise One. She says, 'You know what? You are lovable just as you are. On your deathbed they will say you were a generous and kind soul. You need to feed your body so you can accomplish your goals.'

The Wise One wants me to fill my mind with knowledge that will make a difference in my life, not just the fat grams of what I ate today. Rather than worry about whether I'm the thinnest woman in the room, the Wise One tells me to stop 'competing' and to connect with others on a genuine level.

As Julie connected more fully to her Wise One, she realized she did not want to spend her limited resources on something so unimportant as her weight or her size.

Separating Weight and Goals

If you want to live to be 101 and achieve your other goals, taking care of your body is essential. Being at peace with your body and your weight is different from making weight loss your life goal.

Some of you may identify with Kim, a successful professional woman who binged her way up to a weight that was very unhealthy and uncomfortable and caused her a lot of inner turmoil. When she pondered the three questions, it took a while before she found an answer that was right for her.

Kim:	"But what if weight loss is my goal?"
Amy:	"Do you mean the goal of your life?"
Kim thought a bit before answering:	"No, not really. One of the things I wanted people to say was that I contributed to their lives in some way. And I saw the importance of my career stretch in front of me. But a Part of me wants to make peace with my body before I reach 101. I want to find a loving resolution to my body image issues."
Amy:	"What would happen if you found that loving resolution to your body image issues?"
Kim:	"I hope that I would eat like a normal eater, that I would stop bingeing and be at peace with food."
Amy:	"What do you imagine happening if you could do that?"
Kim:	"I imagine that my body would respond in a healthy way. I imagine that it would start to lose weight all by itself."
Amy:	"Saying 'I want to make peace with my body and find a loving resolution to my body image issues' is very different than saying, 'The goal of my life is to lose 50 pounds.'"
Kim:	"To be honest, I want my struggle with my weight and my body to be a part of what people say about me. I want to be remembered for having tackled something that was my own personal demon, for facing it head on and finding a resolution. Whether it means I'm thin or not, I'd like to be known for being at peace with it."

Amy:	"What you are saying doesn't really have anything to do with weight at all. It's about being at peace within."
Kim:	"I want to be able to do whatever it is that brings me to peace."

When Kim clarified her actual goals, she realized that she had confused losing weight with being at peace with her Self and her body. Resolving her personal demons needed to come from a place of inner wisdom. She also accepted that resolving these demons would guide her body to its own natural healthy weight.

Some of you may also identify with Gabriela who struggled with feelings of remorse about her eating disorder.

Gabriela:	"I have wasted so much of my life dealing with this stupid eating disorder! I'm never going to get these years back. What a waste!"
Amy:	"Gabriela, take a deep breath and step into the Curiosity and Compassion of your Wise One. Then ask that Remorseful Part what it is trying to tell you?"
Gabriela is quiet for a moment before answering:	"It wants me to live my life. It doesn't want me to waste any more time. It wants me to be done – recovered – today."
Amy:	"Oh, it would be nice if you could just recover today. Take a deep breath. Listen to what the Wise One wants to tell you about this."
Gabriela closes her eyes and takes a deep breath. After a moment, her face relaxes and she looks calmer:	"She's just smiling at me. She doesn't feel bad about what we've been through. She looks proud of me."
Amy:	"Ask her what is she proud of?"
Gabriela:	"That I found my Self again. I needed to go through hell in order to get my Self back. For so many years I just existed; I just did what others wanted me to do. But now I can live my life for me. Now that I have Me back, I can make my life have real meaning."

I shared with Gabriela that I view an eating disorder as our journey to learn some important lessons or to gain some important insight about our lives. Although, when we are in the middle of the journey, it is difficult to see the purpose of the struggle. When we learn these important lessons and apply them to our lives, the years spent on that journey are not wasted.

Getting on with Life

Michelle had an "Aha!" moment that changed how she viewed her eating disorder and helped her rediscover meaning in her life. She was in an Intensive Outpatient Treatment program and was very comfortable with the staff and the other members. She couldn't imagine ever wanting to leave.

Each week the program participants took a field trip to challenge them with real-life experiences. One particular week they went to the circus. Before the show began, the Emcee announced the various children's groups present for the performance: "Please welcome Girl Scout Troop 465!" Applause! "Please welcome Parkview Montessori Preschool!" Applause! Michelle started to panic. A Part of her dreaded that they would announce, "Please welcome X Hospital's Eating Disorder Treatment Program!" (Of course they didn't.)

At that moment it hit her, "What am I doing sitting here in the middle of the day at the circus? I need to be getting on with my life!" She suddenly realized that she did not want to identify herself by her eating disorder any longer.

In therapy that week she told me, "I don't want to just be the skinny anorexic girl anymore! I don't really know who I am inside, and it's scary to think of letting it go. But I know it's time for me to move forward. I want to do whatever I have to do to let go of the eating disorder and find myself again."

Finding the Spiritual Side of Recovery

You may find this exercise helps you get in touch with the spiritual side of recovery, whatever that means to you. As you fill the emptiness inside, you may reconnect to nature, the energy of the universe, God or a higher power, or the bigger picture of life.

Jackie, who was in therapy for binge-eating disorder, had a profound experience that dramatically changed how she viewed her body and her eating disorder. She and her mother hiked a pilgrimage trail through Spain. As they backpacked from town to town, enduring heat, rain, steep terrain, and hardship, Jackie was amazed at what her mind and body could do. Not being fluent in the language, she had to rely on her creativity and intelligence to communicate to find food and places to sleep each night.

Jackie and her mother had a harrowing experience:

> We were walking through a very rural area and we came upon a pack of dogs. We had to fend them off using our walking sticks! We literally ran for our lives until we came to a shelter. When you are running for your life, it's very easy to forget about your jiggly thighs. These are the thighs that ran away from those dogs! Man, I am so grateful for these thighs!

Jackie continued:

> Now when I get upset because something is not going right in my life, I say to myself, 'You're not being attacked by a pack of wild dogs. You can handle it!' And that puts it in perspective! I don't let things get me as upset as I used to! I'm so much calmer now than before.

I encourage you to live each day to the fullest, mindful of what is really important to you. Look at your answers to the questions from the exercise earlier in the chapter. On a daily basis, how can you live life according to your values? What can you do to become mindful of what is really important to you in the long run? What thoughts and behaviors do you need to replace because they do not help you to achieve your goals? What are you learning about your Self and about Life that you couldn't learn in any other way?

In the next chapter we'll put what you've learned all together so you can apply it to your everyday life.

Questions to Enhance Your Personal Recovery

Find a quiet time and some privacy to ponder the following questions. You may want to journal what you learn about yourself. I encourage you to share your answers with your therapist.

1 When reading this chapter, did any Parts pop up for you? How were you able to ask them to step aside and allow you to get back into Self-energy?
2 What did the Parts that popped up want to tell you? What did they need from your Wise One Within?
3 Write down the answers to the three questions here.

    a
    b
    c

4   Think of one of your most important values. What is something you could do every day to remind you of that value? How can you live consistently with that value?
5   How do you want to spend your time, energy, money, and intelligence in order to make your life feel meaningful?

Reference

D'Urso-Fischer, Elisa (1999) *Beware of New Year's Resolutions: Empowering Yourself to Change.* The Awakening Center: http://www.awakeningcenter. net/1999.html

9 Making It Work for You

Here you are at the last chapter. So far you've learned that your eating disorder is actually not about food, eating, weight, or your body. The eating disorder symptoms and behaviors are coping mechanisms you learned to deal with your emotions, thoughts, and body sensations after your Self was sacrificed.

You may have begun to figure out why your Self was sacrificed. Which situations, events, issues, and relationships in your past made it unsafe or unacceptable for you to be your Self? If you've been answering the questions and practicing the exercises, you may already have started to feel a firmer sense of Self, of your Wise One Within.

Furthermore, you've learned that your eating disorder is not just one Part. Rather, the various eating disorder behaviors, emotions, thoughts, and beliefs originate from all of your Parts and their relationships to one another when they are extreme.

You may now be more aware of your Parts and their reactions to various situations in your everyday life. You may find yourself breathing into your Wise One Within whenever your Parts react. You may also notice that you are more aware of what your Parts need from your Self when they are triggered.

Last, you've looked at the bigger picture of your life. You stepped back and re-examined what has true meaning and value to you. And – no surprise – you learned that it wasn't food, eating, weight, or the size and appearance of your body.

But, you might wonder, "What do I do with all that I've read so far? How do I apply this to my life?"

Food Issues Are Just Parts

Throughout this book you've become used to thinking of yourself as having many Parts. But it's very common to think that feelings, thoughts, judgments, and beliefs about food, eating, weight, and your body are different – that these are coming from someplace else, and have nothing to do with your Parts.

What may add to the confusion is that your Parts may think, feel, and act differently when you are around food. These feelings, thoughts, judgments, and beliefs are merely the way your Parts have learned to communicate their needs to you. For example, if you are afraid to let go of rigid structure and trust your body and its signals, this is probably a fearful Exile. When you judge or criticize your eating, this is undoubtedly a Bully. Perhaps you get frustrated and say, "Screw it! I'm just going to eat [or starve]!" – that's a Troublemaker. If you resist planning ahead so you will have what you need to take care of your Self and your body, that's a Part. Even telling yourself that your body is somehow different or defective and you cannot eat like a "normal person," well that's just a Part too.

Accessing the Wise One Within

All eating-disorder situations boil down to the lessons you've learned throughout this book. The first step is to access your Wise One Within. Remember the analogy of the junior-high band without a teacher? We need to consciously and consistently keep the teacher in the band room. Then all our Parts can calm down and work together cooperatively and in harmony.

So, how do you keep the teacher in the band room? How do you consciously and consistently live your life as your Self, as your Wise One? First, I encourage you to slow down your life and to develop a daily ritual that can help you access your Wise One Within. If you practice this ritual while you are calm, it will eventually become natural for you to use it when your Parts are triggered.

Like Elece's morning ritual described in Chapter 4, you can begin with something as simple as a few deep calming breaths. You can combine this with reassuring phrases, poems, mantras, and prayers. Picturing your loving Wise One Within can deepen this experience. Linking this experience to an object or a color can be a reminder to practice this throughout the day.

Check in with yourself right now. See if you can find some of the C qualities of Self. For example, deep breathing will bring you to Calmness. Focus on the loving Compassion in your heart. Allow yourself to get Curious about what your Parts will tell you today. Step back and see your situation with your Capacity for objectivity. (Remember, watch out for critical or condemning – that's a Bully!)

Noticing Your Parts

Next, you need to get used to thinking of every feeling, thought, and sensation as merely one of your Parts trying to tell you something or asking for help. In time, you will become adept at slowing down enough to become aware of what you are feeling or thinking in the moment.

Whenever you have a feeling, thought, or reaction, stop and find the Part that needs your help. Calmly, from Curiosity and the loving Compassion of the Wise One Within, focus on that Part and ask, "What Part is that? What does that Part want to tell me? What is this Part trying to do for me? What does that Part need from my Wise One Within?"

As you listen to the Part from your Self, you will spontaneously feel appreciation for the Part's positive intention for you. Intuitively you will know what the Part needs from you. Also, no surprise, you'll find that it isn't about food, eating, weight, or your body.

As your Parts calm down, it will be easier for you to focus on one Part without all the others getting triggered and reacting as well. If another Part cannot step back, your Wise One Within will know that it needs your loving attention too, and you will know you need to ask the same questions you asked the first Part.

"It's Not about Food"

Let's look at some examples that start out being about food, eating, weight, or your body, but eventually reveal what is really going on deep inside. Here, again, is a typical session with Bethany. Her stomach growled loudly at the beginning of a therapy session.

Bethany:	"I'm sorry. I should have eaten before I came, but I just couldn't."
Amy:	"What happened?"
Bethany:	"I know I'm supposed to eat when I am hungry, but sometimes I just feel like I don't deserve to eat."
Amy:	"Bethany, take a breath. Go inside and find the Part that feels that you don't deserve to eat. Focus on how you experience that."
Bethany:	"It's the Little Girl. She doesn't want to eat because another Part tells her she shouldn't want to eat. She shouldn't be hungry. She shouldn't even need to eat. She doesn't deserve food."
Amy:	"Take a breath and go into the Wise One Within. Look at the Little Girl. How do you feel about her or towards her?"
Bethany takes a deep breath and closes her eyes:	"I just want to take care of her. I want to protect her. I feel angry that she gets hurt so often."
Amy:	"Do you get angry at the Little Girl that she gets hurt or at the people who hurt her?"
Bethany:	"Oh no! Not at her. At others."
Amy:	"Ask the Angry One to step aside. The Angry One can be right there, like a Bodyguard."
	Bethany closes her eyes for a moment, and then nods.

Amy:	"Bethany, focus your attention back on the Little Girl and ask her if there is anything else she doesn't deserve."
Bethany:	"She feels she shouldn't need or want anything. She shouldn't be an imposition or a burden to others. She feels she doesn't deserve attention, or affection, or love. She shouldn't ask for anyone to help her."
Amy:	"How does she feel when she's telling you this?"
Bethany:	"She's overwhelmed and very afraid. She doesn't feel like she can handle everything but she thinks she should. She can't do it, and yet can't ask for help because she is so afraid that others will be disappointed in her."
Amy:	"Bethany, go back to the feeling of wanting to take care of her, of protecting her."
	Bethany breathes in, closes her eyes and sits silently. After a while a peaceful look settles on her face. "I told her that she doesn't have to handle everything all by herself. I can help her. I told her that the other Parts, even the Bodyguard, want to help her too. I told her that it's OK to need help; it's OK to ask me to help her and even to ask other people to help. Everybody needs help sometimes."
Amy:	"How is she taking this? What is her reaction?"
Bethany:	"She asked me if I was sure." [Bethany switches to speaking to the Little Girl.] "Yes, honey. I'm sure. I love you and you don't have to be perfect to be loved!"
Amy:	"So what do you want to do about feeding her?"
Bethany:	"Well, she's really hungry. I have a protein bar in my purse. Would you mind if I ate now?"
Amy:	"Yes, of course. You need to let the Little Girl know that it is normal to get hungry and that we need to feed our Body whenever it tells us to. As you eat, notice how the Little Girl feels and reacts."
Bethany takes a bite and closes her eyes as she chews:	"She feels taken care of. She feels loved."
Amy:	"Whenever you notice that it's a struggle to eat when you are hungry, you need to remember that it's the Young Part who doesn't think she should have needs of any kind. As soon as you recognize this feeling, breathe into your Wise One and tell the Little Girl that she deserves to be taken care of. And then feed her from your loving Wise One."

"It's Not about Weight"

Let's look at another example. This one starts out being about weight and eventually reveals active Parts. Hillary was at the point in her recovery that she decided that purging was no longer an option. But she repeatedly weighed herself to calm her intense fear of gaining weight. During our sessions she always took a large pillow and held it in her lap, as if to shield her body from view.

Amy:	"Hillary, get in touch with the Part that is afraid of gaining weight. Find that feeling in your Body. What does that Part want you to know?"
Hillary closes her eyes and sinks down into the couch:	"If I let myself want something I won't be able to control it. I'll end up eating, I'll gain weight. Eating will just make me fat. And then I just want to purge so bad!"
Amy:	"OK, let's just go with that as if it were true. If you did not purge and gained weight, what does the Part want me to know about that?"
Hillary:	"Everyone will see."
Amy:	"If everyone sees, what does the Part think would happen?"
Hillary:	"Everyone will find out . . . ." Her voice trails off.
Amy softly:	"What? What would they find out?"
Hillary, in a very small voice:	"That I'm nothing. That I'm just not good enough. They will know that, deep inside, I'm worthless."

Hillary's intense fear of getting fat, especially now that she was not purging, was not about her weight. Rather, it reflected the core beliefs held by a Young Part. As long as the Young Part believed that she was inherently worthless, Hillary would always fear gaining weight because "fatness" would expose her deepest shame to everyone. Unless Hillary helped the Young Part heal her core beliefs, she would continue to purge and her eating disorder would still control her life.

Amy:	"Hillary, take a deep breath and put the Part that feels worthless in front of you. Take another deep breath and step into your loving Wise One."
Hillary closes her eyes, takes a few deep breaths:	"It's me as a Little Girl. She's just sitting there all alone."
Amy:	"How do you feel towards the Little Girl?"
Hillary:	"I just want to scoop her up in my arms and make her feel better."

Amy:	"Would that be OK with the Little Girl? Would she want you to do that?"
Hillary:	"Yes, but she's afraid that I won't like her. That she is too needy, that she's too much."
Amy:	"How do you feel about that? Do you feel she's too needy, too much?"
Hillary:	"Oh no! She's fine just as she is."
Amy:	"Do you feel she's worthless? That she's not good enough?"
Hillary hugs the pillow and gently strokes it like a child's back. She switches to talking to the Little Girl:	"Oh Honey, no. You're good enough. You're worthy."
Amy:	"How is she responding to this?"
Hillary:	"She's relaxing a bit. She keeps asking, 'Really?'"
Amy:	"Well what do you want to tell her?"
Hillary:	"Yes, really! You're good enough. I love you."

Every time Hillary became anxious that she was gaining weight, she recognized it as a signal that the Little Girl needed reassurance. Hillary would take several deep breaths and, picturing the Little Girl, would say over and over, "You are good enough. You are worthy. You are lovable. I love you."

In time, Hillary noticed that the frequency and intensity of this fear faded. She began to feel more and more comfortable in her Body. As she listened to her Body's signals for hunger, thirst, fullness, rest and movement, her Body began to return to its natural weight. Previously Hillary had "felt huge" at her natural weight, now she felt good enough, worthy, and lovable.

"It's Not about Eating"

In this last example you will notice that all three Parts are active. Kayla is a college student who originally came to therapy for help with compulsive overeating. She was making a lot of progress understanding her Parts until she went home for the winter holidays.

When she walked in the door, her father looked astonished. Taking her aside, he told Kayla that he was very concerned about her health and suggested that Kayla go on a diet and renew her membership at the gym. When Kayla came back to Chicago, her bingeing was out of control again.

Kayla:	"I can't control it. There's something wrong with my body. I just can't eat like a normal person. I'm such a failure. I'm never going to lose weight. Look at me, I'm huge! Who would hire me looking like this!? Who would go out with me!?"

Amy:	"Kayla, I hear your Parts are pretty active right now. I think we need to ask the Wise One to step in. Take a few deep breaths and see if you can find her."
Kayla:	"I'm having a hard time hearing her right now. The Harsh Voice is so loud."
Amy:	"Maybe if it feels heard it will calm down. So let's ask the Harsh Voice what it's trying to do for you right now."
Kayla speaking as the Harsh Voice:	"I want Kayla to lose weight so she can get ahead in life. I want her to date and be in a relationship. I want her to get a job and everything she wants out of life."
Amy:	"And what would that do for Kayla?"
Kayla's voice softens:	"Well, then her life would have meaning. It wouldn't be a waste."
Amy:	"And what would that do for Kayla?"
Kayla in a soft voice:	"She would like herself and be at peace."
Amy:	"Kayla, did you hear that? Do you want that too?"
Kayla:	"Yeah I do."
Amy:	"So just let the Harsh Voice know that you want that too. Can you appreciate what the Harsh Voice is trying to do for you?"
Kayla:	"Yeah, but it makes me feel like a big loser. It's right. I'm never going to get what I want. So why bother?"
Amy:	"What happens when you feel like a big loser and say 'why bother?'"
Kayla's voice gets angry:	"Well I just want to eat. At least food brings me some pleasure. It makes everything feel better. And food doesn't judge me."
Amy:	"Kayla, another Part just stepped in. It sounds angry. What does the Angry Part want you to know?"
Kayla:	"Screw it! Nothing I do is good enough anyway. I am just a big disappointment. I can see it in his eyes, even when he's not making comments."
Amy:	"Whose eyes? Who's making comments?"
Kayla:	"My dad. He never tells me I'm a good student. He never says he's proud of my accomplishments. He only comments about my weight and tells me to go to the gym."
Amy:	"So ask the Angry Part what it's trying to do for you."
Kayla:	"I'll show him! He can't hurt me! I'll be a bigger disappointment."

Amy:	"Kayla, I hear this Part is using food instead of words to tell your dad how you actually feel. If you didn't use food, if you used your words, what would you say to him?"
Kayla:	"I'm mad! You don't see the real me! You only see the outside of me. You don't even know me. I am so much more than my weight."
Amy:	"If you could actually say that to your dad, what would that do for you?"
Kayla:	"I would feel like someone finally stood up for me. Someone finally knew how bad I was feeling inside."
Amy:	"Kayla, I noticed a switch to another Part, a Part that feels bad inside. Focus on that Part. Who is that?"
Kayla:	"It's just a little Girl who feels she's not supposed to speak up. She isn't important. She doesn't know why Daddy ignores her."
Amy:	"How do you feel about her? Is she important to you? Do you want to hear what she has to say?"
Kayla:	"Of course I want to hear her! Just because she's a girl, doesn't mean she's not important. My dad can be such a chauvinist! I want to tell her that her Daddy is wrong!"
Amy:	"Kayla, how is she responding to that?"
Kayla:	"She feels more supported. With me speaking for her, she feels more important."
Amy:	"Kayla, how are you doing now? Do you feel like you will binge today?"
Kayla:	"Actually I'm feeling pretty strong. I feel like all my Parts are working together again."

Kayla became aware that all three of her Parts were trying to tell her something. The Harsh Voice (a Mentor who had slipped back into an extreme Bully role) really wanted Kayla to be healthy and to get everything she wanted in life. But the harshness of that Part triggered an Exile who felt not good enough, not important, and unlovable. An Angry Troublemaker used food to rebel against the Harsh Voice and to soothe the Exile.

Whenever Kayla had the urge to binge she breathed into the loving presence of the Wise One Within. When she did that – like the teacher returning to the junior-high band room – her Parts would become quiet and calm down almost immediately. With Compassion, she listened to each of her Parts and "heard" what they needed to tell her and asked what they needed from her. Eventually, the urge to binge came less and less often and was easier and easier to calm down.

In therapy I warned her, "Your family may not recover along with you." In our sessions together, Kayla needed to practice speaking up to her father in an assertive manner, telling him what she needed to say, so she wouldn't have to turn to food. She also planned out coping skills for when she visited her father, so that when he fell into his critical patterns, she knew how to protect the Little Girl within.

It Is about Food

You've heard me say repeatedly that your eating disorder is not about food, eating, weight or your body. But now I am going to contradict myself. There are aspects of your recovery that are very much about food, eating, weight, and your body.

One aspect of your recovery will be re-learning how to eat normally, naturally, and intuitively. You may remember what "normal eating" was like before you had your eating disorder. Or it may be that it has been such a very, very long time that you don't remember what it was like to eat like a "normal eater." (If only we could observe those "normal eaters" hiding in the mountains of Idaho!)

Another aspect of your recovery will be learning to trust your body and its signals for hunger, fullness, thirst, rest, and movement again. You were born knowing when you were hungry and when you had eaten enough. But, when you sacrificed your Self and cut yourself off from your emotions, you stopped feeling them or you ignored your body signals.

As you become more and more centered in your Self, you will develop trust in your body as well. When you are in touch with the Wise One Within, you will naturally listen to your body's signals and to give it what it needs. You will find that your body doesn't want to binge, nor does it want to starve. Your body naturally wants to move and also needs to rest. And you will find the balance that's right for you, for your body.

Relearning Five Points of Recovery

There are five points that you will need to relearn. They will sound very familiar. You may have already tried multiple ways to "fix" your food, eating, and weight. Like I said in Chapter 1, you can't fix only the eating, food, and weight. But now that you are more at peace with your Self and your Parts, you will be able to get your eating, food, and weight back in balance.

Notice as you read each point what happens inside of you. As thoughts, emotions or sensations arise, remind yourself that these are just Parts who need the loving attention of your Wise One Within. You already know how to calm down your Parts. Breathe into Calmness, Compassion, and Curiosity. Ask the Part what it needs you to know and what it needs and wants from you.

Applying this information means taking what you've learned and turning it into action: making changes in your food, eating, and weight. These changes will probably stir up a lot of thoughts, emotions, and sensations. I highly recommend finding a therapist and a nutritionist who have training and experience with eating disorders and can support and encourage you. You may share this book with them so they understand how to help you stay in your Self and calm down your Parts.

I also highly recommend having a medical doctor on your treatment team. It is extremely common to experience gastrointestinal distress during recovery. It is almost as if the body needs to re-learn how to digest food, especially if you abuse laxatives or purge several times every day. Your doctor can help wean you off laxatives and suggest treatment to make your symptoms easier for you to tolerate. Please be patient and remind yourself "This too shall pass" during these painful periods of recovery. Your body will get back to normal again eventually.

1. "I Eat When I am Hungry"

This sounds simple, but it's actually fairly complex. This point means that you are able to slow down your life enough to pay attention to and listen to your body and recognize its signals for hunger. These signals are different for everybody, for every body. These signals are going to vary among situations, the particular day, the month, or season.

This point also involves accepting your body's need to eat food. No matter how much you want, or no matter how hard you try, you cannot, you will not transcend your body's need for nourishment. You need to become comfortable with having hunger, acknowledging your body's nutritional needs, and allowing yourself to eat each and every time your body becomes hungry. When you eat regularly, bingeing will decrease because your body will no longer be starving. When you eat regularly, gastrointestinal issues will heal. Eventually your body will get back into balance.

2. "I Eat a Wide Variety of Foods"

This point means that you are able to ask your body what it wants to eat and then choose foods accordingly. You are also able to give yourself total permission to choose from any food at all. All foods are equal, there are no "bad" or "good" foods. Your nutritionist can help you with the process of "legalizing" foods.

This point may scare you because you may be in the habit of asking, "What do I have a taste for?" or "What looks good?" Asking your tongue or your eyes can trigger the Child on Your Tongue, a Young Part who wants to eat anything and everything.

When you ask your body, you are actually asking the Wise One Within, not your tongue or your eyes. Her answers will feel calm, clear, and compassionate. Like a loving parent, the Wise One Within knows that your body doesn't feel good when it is given anything and everything. The Wise One Within knows your body needs nutritious foods, prepared in ways that taste good. While, at the same time, the Wise One also knows the Child on Your Tongue deserves occasional fun treats.

Personally, I believe we were meant to have fun and enjoy each day. Therefore, we should eat something fun and enjoyable every day as well.

3. *"I Eat in a Way That Enhances Stopping When I Am Full"*

People have already told you, "Just stop when you are full!" You've already tried it, so you know that it can be very difficult. Eating in a way that enhances stopping when full is different from "just stopping." You may already be aware that when you eat mindlessly, you experience very little satisfaction, and because you are not satisfied, you begin to hunt for more food to eat.

What is satisfaction? It is eating foods that match what your body wants and needs, and is food prepared in ways that are enjoyable for the Child on Your Tongue. When you savor an enjoyable meal that "hits the spot," that's satisfaction.

When you eat mindfully, you can heighten your feelings of satisfaction. When you slow down your eating, you can listen to your body's signals for fullness. You may find that, when you eat slowly and mindfully, you actually eat less than you did before.

But, it is very important to note, a Part of you may try to turn eating slowly and mindfully into a weight-loss tactic. After almost three decades of helping people recover, I firmly believe weight loss as a goal is incompatible with recovery from an eating disorder. Each time you ignore your body's signals for hunger, skip a meal, or restrict the types or the amounts of food you eat, you dig yourself further into your eating disorder.

If this happens, simply breathe into the Wise One Within, and ask for her help getting your Parts back on track (and, of course, also ask for help from your therapist and nutritionist).

4. *"I Forget about It Afterwards and Get On with my Life"*

"Normal" eaters don't think about what they've eaten, even when they've eaten too much. They may rub their stomachs and moan, "Oh I ate too much!" But then they go cut the grass, work on the computer, call a friend, get on with their lives.

How are they able to do this? They have what I call "body trust." They know their body, they trust that their body will digest whatever they've eaten and eventually get back to hunger again. If they have over-eaten, they know that it just takes longer for their body to return to hunger. Also, while they are waiting to get back to hunger, they don't think about it, and they don't beat themselves up.

In order to learn body trust, you have to allow yourself to experience and tolerate fullness – and allow your body to get back to hunger naturally. This means making a commitment to not purge. When you know you can purge, you tell yourself, "Since I'm going to purge, I might as well keep on eating anything and everything I want." Once you commit to making purging no longer an option, your binges will automatically get smaller.

I assure you, every feeling, emotion, and body sensation will pass eventually. Until you are used to allowing these feelings and sensations to progress naturally, your Scared Parts will need plenty of soothing, encouragement, and guidance from your Wise One Within. The help and support of your therapist and nutritionist can be invaluable during this process.

5. "I Accept, Love, and Appropriately Move the Body I Was Given Genetically"

There are several important aspects to this point. Let's do the easier one first – moving your body appropriately. When you listen to your body's signals, you will hear how often your body wants to move. Your body wants to dance, jump, skip, swim, almost every day – but not all day.

You also must learn to respect your body's need for rest and rejuvenation. Think of your cell phone. If you don't recharge the battery, you will not be able to make calls, text, or use any apps. The same is true with your body. If a Part of you becomes anxious thinking about resting, you now know what to do: Breathe into the Wise One Within, and calmly and compassionately soothe the Anxious Part.

A harder aspect of this point is seeing your body as acceptable and lovable – as it is right now in this very moment. This is difficult because you are constantly bombarded with messages that, no matter what you look like, it isn't good enough.

Allow me to step up on my soapbox for a moment. Our culture is moving towards acceptance of diversity: race, religion, ethnicity, sexual orientation, and physical disability. But it still does not accept that people come in a wide variety of body types and sizes. It does not tell you that all body types and sizes can be beautiful. Society tells you over and over that if you try hard enough, you can – and must – change your body type in order to be beautiful, even though research shows that about 85 percent of what you look like is genetic.

In order to accept and love your body, you must catch, stop, and challenge every body-hating thought. If hating your body actually cured your eating disorder or changed your basic body type, then you would already be recovered, in a thin and "ideal" body. Body-hating thoughts just make all your Parts feel worse – much, much worse – and then they resort to their eating disorder symptoms. So you must admit that hating your body doesn't work.

Body hatred is based on a distorted body image, the picture you have in your mind of what you think you look like, combined with all the judgments and criticisms that go along with this. You are disconnected from what you actually look like to all the people in your life. Distorted body image stems from negative core beliefs held by your Kid Parts and are actually not about your body.

Let's look at one more example that shows that the origins of body hatred are actually not about your body. Jaime, whom you met briefly at the beginning of Chapter 7, came to therapy because of her problems with binge eating. Having studied theater and dance in college, she was a naturally exuberant person, with an animated spirit that I found delightful. Her large round curvy body glowed with an inner beauty that she had trouble seeing.

Ever since she was a small child, if Jaime was anxious or upset, a very loud, strong voice inside would automatically shout, "You're Stupid, Fat, and Ugly!" This made her feel hopeless and worthless. Then a Numbing Troublemaker took over and turned to eating, sleeping or watching TV.

Amy:	"Jaime I know you're having a really tough time with body image right now. Let's listen to the Critical Part. If he feels heard, he may calm down."
Jaime:	"He says I'm stupid, fat, and ugly and no one will ever love me."
Amy:	"Does he sound like anyone you know?"
Jaime:	"My dad used to tell me, 'If you weren't so fat! Quit being so dramatic! Shut up! Don't be so loud!' I always felt like I was too much for him. I tried to trim myself back because I felt like I was too big, too loud, just too Too! I just knew I was unlovable because I was so fat."
Amy:	"So the Critical Part is just echoing what your dad used to say to you. What is the Critical Part trying to do for you?"
Jaime as the Critical Part:	"I'm trying to make her be smaller inside and out. Then someone will love her and she will feel safe and secure, and be at peace."
Jaime laughs:	"He is yelling at me so that ultimately I can have peace."
Amy:	"Yes, sometimes our Parts do not make sense. Now find the Part that reacts to the Critical Part."
Jaime:	"It's the Little Girl. She just feels icky. No, she thinks she *is* icky. She believes she is just *bad*! She's scared.

She's wondering, 'What if he is right. What if I *am* too big! What if I *am* too much! What if I *am* stupid, fat, and ugly and no one will love me? What if there's something wrong with me?'"

Jaime's voice gets very young and very sad:
"Everyone's got something lovable about them. If you're not lovable, then something must be wrong with you. I'm just too much for other people. I'm too big. I'm too fat."

Amy:
"Jaime, take a deep breath and step back into the Wise One. Can you see the Little Girl?"
Jaime nods.

Amy:
"Jaime, is she too big? Is she too much? Does she need to trim herself back? Is there something wrong with her? Is she unlovable?"

Jaime shakes her head vigorously, and speaks in a soft voice to the Little Girl:
"No. You're not too much! You're not too big! You're just right. There is just enough of you! You're fine just as you are. You are lovable because *I* love you."

Amy:
"How is she reacting?"

Jaime:
"She feels so relieved. She's calm again."

Amy:
"Jaime, have the Wise One tell the Critical Part how his comments make the Little Girl feel."

Jaime takes a deep breath and firmly but calmly says:
"You're talking to a Little Girl – she's only 7 years old. You make her feel worthless, like she's something stuck on the bottom of your shoe. You hurt her. You certainly don't make her feel better."

Amy:
"What's his reaction?"

Jaime:
"He said, 'I'm sorry.' Like he never thought of that before. [Jaime continues speaking calmly to the Critical Part] I appreciate that you want me to be a better person, happy, loved, and content. But I don't see how buying into the Barbie-doll mentality that I have to be thinner or prettier makes me a better person. Let's look at the stuff that really matters."

Amy:
"Jaime, this Part's positive intention is to make the Little Girl be safe, secure and at peace. Since he's been calling you 'stupid, fat, and ugly' for over 30 years, it's going to take a while before he gets used to saying something else. You'll have to practice different phrases until something clicks for both of you."

Jaime, a big smile appearing on
"'Danger Will Robinson!' Like the robot on the old TV show, 'Lost in Space.'"

her face as
she waves
her arms in
the air:

Amy: "Great! You've started a new relationship with him now. Remember you are now on the same team. You'll have to practice. If he slips and says 'stupid, fat, and ugly,' please stop, take a deep breath, and remind him to say, 'Danger Will Robinson!'"

When Jaime came back the next week, she was excited to report on her progress.

Jaime: "I noticed throughout the week that I was able to catch myself. Sometimes that Part got to 'You're stup . . .' and I would catch it and make him say, 'Danger Will Robinson!'"

Amy: "Hmmmm, I wonder why he says, 'Danger!'?"

Jaime: "I noticed he announces danger when I am feeling something uncomfortable, fear, anger, sadness, pretty much any emotion he sees as dangerous, overwhelming. And if I'm overwhelmed I will be inundated with feelings and I won't be able to function. I won't get off the couch, or hold down a job. I'd lose my apartment. I'd have to move back in with my parents again!"

Amy: "Well if that were to happen, that would be unpleasant indeed. Let's see if we can work with these feelings to see what they need from you."

Jaime and I worked with all of her Parts to see what they needed from her Self. As they learned to trust the Wise One Within, they calmed down and were triggered less often. She felt more comfortable in her body and, as a result, she binged less often. Because of that, her body slowly, slowly started to go to the weight it was meant to be. Jaime felt good at this weight even though it was rounder and curvier than the "ideal" body type currently lauded by society.

Whenever you feel too fat, too big, or too much, breathe into your Wise One Within. Calmly, with loving Compassion and Curiosity ask, "What Part of me feels too big or too much?" With Courage ask, "Too much for who? Why are they uncomfortable with my 'big-ness,' with my 'much-ness'?"

Your Wise One Within can lovingly help you accept that this is the body you have today – even if it is currently at a higher weight than it was meant to be. The Wise One can help you appreciate all that your body does for you each and every day. If your body is larger than it was meant to be, as you recover it will slowly, slowly (and you cannot speed up the process) go to its healthy weight.

Your Recovery Will Not Be Perfect

You need to expect your recovery to have its ups and downs. You will have a few days of success and then you may fall back and use your eating disorder behaviors again. This will happen over and over again during your recovery process. You may get discouraged and a Part may think, "I can't do this. I'm never going to recover!"

But slips and lapses are an inevitable part of recovery. Each time you fall back and binge, purge, over-exercise, or starve yourself, rather than seeing it as a failure you can think of it as an opportunity to learn about your Self and your Parts.

I want to share with you some advice I received from my therapist when I was in a particularly discouraged place in my recovery journey. She drew a line on a piece of paper (Figure 9.1) and said, "This is what you think recovery looks like."

Then she drew another line (Figure 9.2) and said, "This is what recovery actually looks like."

She drew a circle at the bottom of one of the down points of the line and said, "This is where you are now. But look! After every down point is a period of growth. You're on the verge of another upswing in your recovery!"

So, when you have a down point in your recovery, breathe into your Wise One Within and look at the lapse with Curiosity and Compassion. Ask yourself, "What was that about? What were my Parts trying to do for me? What did my Parts need from me?" Step back and through your Capacity for Objectivity ask yourself, "If this exact event happened to a friend what would I say to her? What would I suggest she do instead of using behaviors?"

Reach out to your therapist, your nutritionist or to a supportive friend. Ask them to help you make a plan for the next time you feel like falling back on your eating disorder behaviors. Write the plan down on a card and keep this plan with you.

There's No Magic Diet

You may still notice a Part who wants me to just give you a Magic Diet – exactly what to eat, how much to eat, and when to eat it – so that you don't gain any weight. In fact this Part may still want you to lose a few more pounds.

Just to reiterate, weight loss as a goal is INCOMPATIBLE with recovery from an eating disorder.

There is no Magic Diet (sorry to disappoint you). Even if there were one, I wouldn't give it to you. First, how would this Magic Diet know

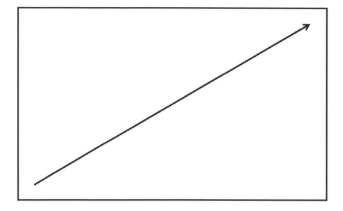

Figure 9.1 Imagined graph of recovery.

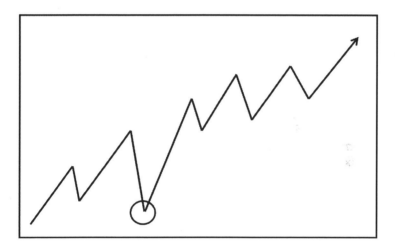

Figure 9.2 Realistic graph of recovery.

what you and your body need? Your body's nutritional needs change daily, sometimes hourly.

Second, diets just encourage you to live by rules that are set by someone else. That's the opposite of living your life in your own Self-energy.

Third, diets do not teach you how to listen to your own body, nor do they help you learn body-trust. Diets are temporary solutions to a bigger problem, and they don't address the underlying issues that make your Parts want to starve, binge, purge, or exercise. Imagine taking a pain reliever for a headache that is really caused by a brain tumor. Also, don't get me started about the feminist implications of keeping women occupied with daily doses of self-hatred and loathing.

While I firmly believe that diets don't work, I do support food plans. A food plan can be an important and supportive tool to use during your recovery. If you are working with a nutritionist, her goal for you is to eventually be able to listen to your own body and to trust that it knows what it needs to be healthy.

As you learn different tools and add them to your recovery toolbox, you'll learn to trust that your Self and your Parts will find harmony with one another. You'll develop body-trust, know what your body's needs are, and how much and how often to feed yourself. (Hmmm, Your Recovery Toolbox. That sounds like the title of my next book!)

There's No Magic Wand

If you look deep within, you may notice you still have a Part who wants to just go to bed and wake up tomorrow completely recovered, without having to do any work. I'm sorry to disappoint you again, but recovery is not quick or easy. If it were, you would have done it years – even decades – ago.

You have to do the work, practice the skills, form new habits, figure out alternatives, heal your core beliefs, and learn new tools to put in your recovery toolbox. When you are recovered, life will not suddenly be perfect. You will continue to have feelings, reactions, and problems. But, because you have Self-energy, your Wise One Within will handle these problems calmly, compassionately, and courageously.

Recovery Is WORTH It

With all this talk about how difficult recovery is, and how long it can take, you may be asking, "Why even bother?" All I can tell you is that everyone I have met who has recovered said it was worth it. They found freedom. They found self-love, self-acceptance, inner peace, and contentment. They finally knew who they were – and they liked that person. They were able to develop satisfying and healthy relationships. They found a deeper purpose and meaning to life, and you will too.

When you get your Self back, you fill the emptiness inside; you find your "much-ness." You discover the Wise One Within and can tap into her Compassion, Curiosity, and Calmness whenever you need her. All of the answers you need are already within you. She is just one breath away.

The Wise One Within knows that it's fine to accept yourself for who you are. It's fine for you to be you, to feel your feelings, think your thoughts, act your actions. Celebrate who you are – you are a unique individual. There is no one like you. You are perfect just as you are.

Just as you can accept the uniqueness of your temperament, talents, and strengths, you can also accept that it's normal to have limitations, inabilities, and weaknesses. You do not have to do everything perfectly in order to be lovable – you already are lovable. You do not have to try to be someone else – you are perfect just as you are.

When you know deep inside that you are good enough, you will be able to connect with others in truly healthy relationships. There are many amazing people out there who will appear in your life when you are ready for them.

The Wise One Within knows your body is unique, and you can celebrate its diversity. You do not have to look like everyone else. Your body is beautiful and lovable already.

The Wise One Within knows you are so much more than your body. It is merely the vehicle that gets you where you want to go in your life. Go back to your answers from the questions in Chapter 8. What do you value? How do you want to live your Life? How do you want others to remember you? You need to love and care for your body so it can last until you are 101 years old.

Commit to Your Recovery

Make a commitment to your recovery. Right now, close your eyes, and ask the Wise One what your body wants from you. Write it down on a card. Put the card somewhere you will see it every day.

Find moments to practice your recovery each day. At first you will need to consciously practice your recovery daily. Learn from each slip and celebrate each success. Soon, with diligence and practice, maintaining your recovery will become second nature to you.

You need to learn how to stop thinking about eating and get on with your life. Take a class, join a club, find a hobby, change careers. Make new friends and reconnect with old ones who have slipped away. There is an amazing amount of richness just waiting for you out there; I encourage you to reach out and grab it.

You are a capable, competent person who has the resources to cope with whatever comes along. Take back your power. Take back your voice. Learn to speak up and even sometimes say, "No!"

Balance self-care with care for others. Step out of yourself and help others, whether you volunteer to build houses for the homeless, help with a political campaign, knit hats for premature babies, or just shovel snow for an elderly neighbor. Giving back to others completes your recovery.

Reconnect with yourself spiritually. Take a walk in nature, look at the stars, meditate, pray – whatever makes you feel connected to something bigger than yourself. You are definitely not alone.

I am excited for you! You have taken many steps on your self-care journey. I encourage you to invite all your Parts to join you.

Namasté,

Amy

Questions to Enhance Your Personal Recovery

Find a quiet time and some privacy to ponder the following questions. You may want to journal what you learn about yourself. I encourage you to share your answers with your therapist.

1   When reading this chapter, did any Parts pop up for you? How were you able to ask them to step aside and allow you to get back into Self-energy?
2   What is a daily ritual you can create to practice accessing your Wise One Within?
3   Notice if you have any feelings or sensations right now. Are any of them C qualities of Self? If any are not C qualities, which Part is active? What does this Part need or what is it trying to tell you?
4   What are ways your body signals hunger to you? What signals do you receive from your body when you are full?
5   What's one way you can make eating a more mindful experience? How can you eat in a way that enhances stopping when full?
6   What are ways your Wise One Within can calm your Parts as you learn to "forget about it and get on with life"?
7   What does "getting on with life" look like for you? What would be a sign that you are "getting on with life"?
8   How will you catch, stop, and challenge your body-hate thoughts?
9   Take some time to make a list of all the new tools in your Recovery Toolbox. Allow yourself to be amazed at all you've learned.

Index

Made in the USA
Las Vegas, NV
13 April 2021